DIALOGUES

AMONGST THE

PEOPLE

CALLED

UNITED METHODISTS

DIALOGUES

AMONGST THE

PEOPLE

CALLED

UNITED METHODISTS

William J. Abraham

HIGHLAND LOCH PRESS
Dallas, TX , USA

DEDICATED

To the memory of the Irish pioneers who first brought
Methodism to North America

Published in association with **Wordsmith Media Inc**.

First edition.

Published by Highland Loch Press,
Dallas, Texas, USA,

ISBN-13: 978-0692255674

Contents

Dialogue I

Opening Gambit

TRADITIONALIST   There is a simple solution. Those who cannot abide by our doctrine and discipline should leave and establish their own denomination. In the process we should hold to church law on the ownership of property. The systematic nullification of church law is what has landed us in this mess in the first place. I see no reason to abandon it now. Those who cannot abide by our doctrine and discipline should leave. They should depart without their property and find their own way in the world.

EVANGELICAL   This is not exactly the start I was hoping for on this sunny morning!

TRADITIONALIST   Hear me out. These self-appointed progressives who are wrecking our church should be called to exercise integrity and face the fact that their game is over. As a reward for what they have been doing they should get a taste of their own medicine for a change. Just look at the litigation in the Episcopal Church; despite the appeal to the high moral ground they are ruthless in disposing of their opponents. They did this in parts of the Presbyterian Church as well, but I will spare you chapter and verse. In the end straight talk and resolute action is the only kind of dialogue these folk understand. The time for pious peace-keeping is long past; we need to take action and take it urgently. There is no need to split. The progressives should show some integrity, leave, and let the rest of us get on with our mission and ministry. We have enough trouble on our hands salvaging the remnants of our tradition and repairing local dysfunctional congregations without having to fight unending battles for the very existence of our church. It is ridiculous beyond words that those who have stood by the teaching and practices of the church

1

should be thinking of leaving. We need to keep our nerve and see this thing through to the finish.

EVANGELICAL   You must have gotten out of the wrong side of the bed this morning. Where is grace, that hallmark of our beloved tradition, in all this?

TRADITIONALIST   You mean you want another pious sermon on cheap grace. You really mean you want another little workout in sentimentality? Where grace means no one has to take responsibility and say they are sorry. Where grace means you can avoid repentance and let the political bullies carry on as before. Where grace means you can change the subject so that the real problem never gets identified much less addressed. And where grace is a dumb, blue-eyed blonde who cannot see the abuse that is being permitted in her name. Listen, we all know that when any major crisis emerges folk use it as an occasion to vent on all the issues they've bottled up for years. The immediate appeal to grace is just a way to calm everybody down and pretend that the real issue is a spiritual one that especially afflicts those who want to get to the obvious and immediate problem that needs attention. One group imagines the problem is those extremists who are drowning out the middle. Another group thinks that the problem is once again our refusal to work off scripture. Another group wants an additional round of holy conferencing. Yet another group wants those terrible conservatives who are standing in the way of progress to leave. The problem is simple. The order of the church is being dismantled by a determined and well-organized minority which has failed to get its way through our standard channels of decision making. They have not just been allowed but have downright been encouraged to keep up the pressure, hoping one day to win by hook or by crook. The solution to this problem is simple. Those who reject the teachings and discipline of our church should just leave.

EVANGELICAL   Calm down my friend. I have as robust a vision of grace as you do. What you fail to realize is that the water has already been spilt and it cannot be gathered up again. You are deeply mistaken if you think that this solution of yours will work. The progressives have no intention of leaving. So what do you have in mind? Sending in the District Superintendents to change the locks? You know full well why they will not leave. First, they will never be able to survive on their own. They are essentially organisms who live off the rest of the body. Apart from a few exceptions they are declining as fast as we can count. Second, their agenda is a full-scale cultural agenda. From the early 80s, if not before, they set out to change the law, the military institutions, and mainline Protestantism. Our church is the last hold-out and they see victory in sight. It is foolish therefore to think we can force them out. That is why I am committed to a more gracious and generous approach. We should acknowledge their integrity and find a way where everyone is a winner and figure out a way to move to amicable separation.

PROGRESSIVE   You know I really resent the way you both describe what we are doing. And I find the reference to dumb blondes hopelessly sexist. Of course, we are engaged in a culture war against bigots and homophobic conservatives like you who are stuck in a time warp, but you pay no attention to the theological arguments that are the core of our position. We are not off to a promising start with this conversation if this is the way we are going to proceed. I thought you people were supposed to be about theology. Immediately you show your real colors by jumping into the deep end of politics from the get-go. And it is clear that the only strategy Traditionalist has is to double down on the legalism that is already killing us. I can assure you that I do not for a moment accept your account of what the problem is. Even more emphatically, I can assure you that we are not leaving.

EVANGELICAL   Believe it or not you and I may be together on the point before us. You have to agree that however you describe Traditionalist's proposal, it is totally impracticable. We need a more generous way forward; contrary to first impressions, amicable separation is the way to go.

TRADITIONALIST   I can make my point just as easily in terms of my theology of the church. The church is not some society of friends but a holy body with a proper order intended to sort through conflicts, preserve its unity, and make possible its vital ministry. Once you undermine that order it will disintegrate. Those who undermine its order are responsible for its disintegration. They should cease and desist or leave and form their own progressive denomination. Moreover, aside from being a silly oxymoron, amicable separation is a pipe-dream. Look at what happened in the 1840s when the Northern and Southern Churches were formed. It was all worked out and agreed until one group decided not to play ball and the whole thing ended up in the Supreme Court of the United States. Rest assured somebody will find a way to throw a legal spanner in the works and then it will be death struggle down to the last candlestick on the last remaining altar. My solution is simpler and cleaner. Your solution is radical and thus betrays its intended conservative instincts. Conservatives are those who conserve the treasures and best practices of the past; it is radicals who want to tear things up and start all over again from scratch. Progressive simply wants to take over the current institutions and let you wither on the vine.

EVANGELICAL   Talk of amicable separation simply sets the right tone. Let's get beyond semantics. I agree that we need action. We need a workable solution and amicable separation is not a pipe-dream. If you baulk at the adjective, then lets simplify speak of separation or division or whatever other noun you prefer. Whatever we name it, it requires cool heads and deft legislation. We can make it happen if there is the will to make it happen. There is no pain-free solution so let's sit down and reason together. Consider this: let's appoint a Commission of the General Conference with the mandate to bring forward legislation to a called session of the General Conference in 2017. We will be ready with our proposals and let others bring theirs and let's hammer this out together.

TRADITIONALIST   I am sure you will be ready but I am unhappy with this whole operation. Too many conservatives, not least the evangelical wing, are unreliable in the long-run. You talk a good talk but you do not have the courage to stand your ground and see things through to the end. For one thing, you provide over time most of the foot-soldiers for the progressive wing of the church. The others arise out of the overheated moralism our tradition all too readily cultivates. For another thing, you have been so intimidated and demonized by the middle and the progressives that many in your fold eventually cave. They end up reiterating the tired and unconvincing arguments developed a generation before by your opponents. You suffer from theological Stockholm syndrome. Now is not the time for further compromise. We are dealing with people who have lost the argument over the last forty years in the only place it counts, that is, our General Conference. So what do they do? They resort to intimidation, bullying, name-calling, political theatre, and the barefaced nullification of our canon law. This is not the religion of reason and methodical order that Wesley taught us. It is the religion of aggressive moralistic intimidation wrapped up in liberal and liberationist preacher talk. It is time we stopped rewarding such behavior and action. These folk are splitting our church from top to bottom; they should leave, found their own denomination, and pay their own bills.

EVANGELICAL   I agree we evangelicals have our wayward children, but this is true of every expression of Christianity. After all, we United Methodists not only believe in backsliding, we also practice it. So we are no better and no worse than other groups who have wandering offspring. I would deny that we are the seed-bed of progressives. We have conserved the riches of our heritage and will continue to do so. I agree, to be sure, that living in a dysfunctional and at times poisonous environment has harmful effects, but we have done the best we can to deal with them. The crucial point is that we have reached an impasse and we now need to find a way forward where we do the least harm. I am prepared to acknowledge the sincerity and authenticity of those who disagree with us. I hope they will do the same with us as their opponents. So what is at issue is not another compromise but a gracious effort to get out of our current stalemate. I know that talk of amicable separation is easy to ridicule; but we are already knee-deep in division and schism. In time folk will get over their current state of denial and face up to the reality we are facing. This is exactly the first step to a resolution that would make amicable separation a live option. Maybe the church as a whole will reject it; but we still need to get beyond denial and get all options out on the table.

TRADITIONALIST   Time, of course, will tell. At present I am totally skeptical precisely because once you begin down that road you will not be able to tame the forces that will be unleashed in the church. They will devour us all.

EVANGELICAL   You have a point. Much will depend on what our progressive opponents decide to do. However, we are offering an olive branch not a poisoned chalice. They should be given a chance to say their piece and defend their position.

PROGRESSIVE   Some of our number will not trust you as far as we could throw you. Since the birth of our church in 1968 you have been nibbling away at its pluralism, inventing nasty interest groups that you dress up as renewal, sabotaging our efforts to bring our church up to speed on the proper reform of our practices related to the discrimination against our LGBTQIA brothers and sisters. Why should we talk to you much less cooperate with you to split our beloved church?

EVANGELICAL   Hold on a minute. I thought you progressives took pride in your commitment to dialogue and holy conferencing. Be honest, now. You have lost the vote over the last forty years and are now making one more last ditch effort to rally the troops for victory in 2016. You are alienated from The United Methodist Church and are angry at the stance it has taken across the years. So there is good news for you here. Let's stop the blame game and finger pointing and set each other free to do what we think God has called us to do. You can walk away with dignity and fulfill the ministry you sincerely believe God has given you to implement. We can walk away and follow the scriptures that are the foundation of all our work. Let's work toward an equitable division of the assets; indeed we will be generous in this arena; for, if truth be told, we are not very enamored of many of the assets. Be that as it may, our desire is to be gracious and magnanimous. Let's declare a draw and move on. Maybe generations to come will say you were right; but for now we are bound to conscience and the Word of God.

Scripture, Accommodation, and Splitting

PROGRESSIVE   I take your point and will do what I can to withhold my suspicions. But let's get one thing straight. Your claim to a monopoly on scripture is entirely bogus. That was a nice version of "You follow your way and we will follow God's way" that you just tried to slip by us all. I know I cannot match your ability to quote scripture verses, but I know my Bible. As you know the issue comes down not just to scripture but to the interpretation of scripture. We also take our stand on scripture. We look to the general principles of scripture in loving our neighbor and in doing justice and these take priority over the biblical materials that generally frown on homosexual practice. We take our stand on a generic canon within the canon. You know, it is hard to stomach your hypocrisy at times. You stand by what you claim is biblical teaching on homosexuality but you long ago abandoned scriptural teaching on divorce and on women in ministry. Your claim to be biblical is really a disguise for your bourgeois and entirely relative adoption of recent family values as the teaching of scripture. You and your friends are in bed with the Republican Party and sold on an economic vision that hurts the poor. Some of your own people are now happily coming over to our side because they cannot stand your nasty, judgmental attitudes and your inconsistent appeal to scripture. And while they are a tad too pious for our liking, we welcome their support in the short-term.

EVANGELICAL   Well of course the issue comes down to in- terpretation. We have never denied this. We simply insist that at the end of the day you have to make up your mind as to what scripture teaches. There is a time and place for debate about what scripture means. We have done our homework on what it means, and now we have reached our decision on this score we take our stand. Like Luther, we say, God help us we can do no other. If this were merely a parochial North American debate then your sociological observation about bourgeois society would have merit. However, this is now a global issue that confronts the entire church across the world. We choose to stand shoulder to

7

shoulder with the church as a whole across space and time. It is you and your friends who have capitulated to the pressure from culture; you are simply accommodating to a culture that has lost its moral bearings since it abandoned the Christian faith in the modern period.

PROGRESSIVE   You are right but only half-right in what you say. On the surface we are the party of accommodation. However, this is a pejorative way to describe our stance. We are the party who believe that the church should revise its doctrines and practices in the light of the best information currently available. If you like, we take far more seriously than you do the place of reason and experience in theology. We rightly adjusted on the interpretation of the early chapters of Genesis, on slavery, on women's ordination, on racial prejudice, and now on the rights of non-heterosexuals to be what God has made them to be. We make no apology for the adjustments we are proposing. And we are exercising our rights as Methodists and Protestants to revise our received tradition. In the end your side comes around and quietly adopts our positions; you are like adolescents; one day you will grow up and see the light. In the meantime, we are no longer going to stand by and be silent any longer.

EVANGELICAL   Once you speak like this, it's abundantly clear why we should be willing to face the question of amicable divorce. Our disagreements go all the way to the top in our doctrine of creation and all the way to the bottom in our vision of sin. In between we differ on the meaning and place of divine revelation in resolving our moral and theological divisions. It is time to call a halt to this debate and move on. There has been enough pain on all sides. We have reached the point where the pain we currently face is much greater than the pain that change will impose upon us. Here's where we are: If you win, we have to walk away in good conscience as informed by our faith. If we continue to win, then we stand in the way of what you honestly consider to be good conscience as informed by our faith. Let's put our heads and hearts together and work for a win-win solution. We propose what is really a centrist position that brings our wars to an end and operates out of a mentality of genuine grace and generosity towards our opponents. I know this is hard to fathom initially but sleep on it and you will see I am right.

PROGRESSIVE   Don't be so patronizing! We have already slept on it and thought about it. We have no desire to be party to any proposal that will split the church. You are the splitters; we are the people of peace, reconciliation, inclusion, and unity.

EVANGELICAL   But you are already splitting the church in practice. Look at all the Annual Conferences where you wear those rainbow stoles to mark off your party as distinct and different from the rest of us. I know you have your extremists and hot-heads like we do. However, aside from the divisive liturgical dress code you have adopted, you are entirely happy to condone the disruption of our regular committees and conferences. Get real and face up to the fact that you are creating a whole new edition of United Methodism and that this already splits the church. Your claim to be the party of unity and peace is the mere repetition of error. Your understanding of reconciliation and inclusion are so loaded with hidden agendas and exclusion that we are no longer fooled by them.

PROGRESSIVE   We are not splitting the church. We are simply following the true and trusted practices that we learned when we dealt with the evil of racism in the civil rights era. Of course, you do not like your comfort zone to be disturbed. Your slave-owning ancestors and racist forbears did not like our disruptive tactics. We are not backing down and will not cease until we bring to an end the bigotry, injustice, and oppression you and your friends represent. History is on our side; the moral arc of history clearly bends clearly in our direction. The younger generation is joining us; we are on the cusp of a mighty victory for liberation in the history of the church.

EVANGELICAL   It is good at last to see you come clean and lean on the broken reed of liberation theology. We all know that is the tacit default ideology of many of our leaders, even if the version is so soft it is virtually invisible. Your claim to distill where history is going is a rerun of the Gnostic claim that somehow you have an inside track on the meaning of history. Your move to apply the old ploy of guilt by association is a tired mantra. And the standard tropes of bigotry and injustice are mere gestures of dogmatism disguised as moral criticism. The church got it wrong on slavery and racism. It did so for complex reasons and interests that were indeed overturned by the deeper truths of our Lord and the Gospel. Do you now want us to make the same mistake all over again and ignore our Lord's clear teaching on marriage that he relates quite specifically to his vision of creation? We prefer to stand with the offense of our Lord than dwell in the courts of Hollywood and the North American elites who are destroying the fabric of our civilization and leading us back into a new Dark Ages.

PROGRESSIVE I cannot believe that you think this way about us. I honestly tried to meet you half-way but all I get is a belly-full of high-brow negativity. Where did you learn to argue in such a contrarian fashion? I certainly never learned to think like this at the seminary I attended; we took much more seriously the transformative and liberating aspects of Christianity.

EVANGELICAL Then maybe your seminary needs a faculty shakeup or maybe you need a recall so you can wrestle with proposals that do not fit your predetermined conclusions. If we keep on speaking like this to one another we are simply moving back to ground zero again. Let's stop the wrangling and move forward to an amicable separation before we both say something we will live to regret. I am sick and tired of the endless wrangling; it is bad for the soul as well as for the work of the church.

A Third Way

RECONCILER Permit me a word in edgeways at this point as you slug it out. Surely you are forgetting the vast number of good United Methodists who are tired of this division into conservatives and progressives. There are three groups and I wish to speak for a third way beyond these disruptive extremes.

TRADITIONALIST You have a strange version of arithmetic in play here. Didn't you notice that I started this conversation? Don't I get to count as well? My count says that there are now four rather than three of us in the conversation.

RECONCILER   Of course you count in the conversation! Everybody does. Stop playing a silly numbers game. When we are done I hope you will join our team and help us all move forward. Let's begin afresh with the numbers. There is a vast middle out there which is as tired of the wrangling. That's why I helped craft a resolution to the last General Conference which would resolve the issue by recording that we disagree on the central issue before us. I know it failed but I have an updated version that I think will work.

TRADITIONALIST   It is good to see you have gotten past asking General Conference to endorse your armchair sociology. The role of General Conference is to make normative decisions on the life and work of the church; this is the only body that can do this and it is what philosophers call a category mistake to ask it to record sociological data. Either you are recording a platitude which is just silly in this arena; or you are using the recording of a platitude to smuggle in a substantive proposal which is cheating. Now that you are out in the open, it is tempting to take the second of these alternatives as the right way of reading your odd appeal to a platitude that no one contests.

RECONCILER   Thanks for the philosophy lesson; I can play that game too, as you will see shortly. We need peace in our church; real peace that will get us out of the impasse we all know exists. Rather than divide, let's deploy the principle of subsidiarity. Let's agree to settle what we will do about the contested issues before us by passing the decisions down first to Annual Conferences and then to local churches. We keep the teaching and practice of the church as it is as our default position. If no-one wants to change let that be their position. However, Annual Conferences can opt out of the general default position by appropriate action and so can local churches. Each can resolve the matter before them by majority or super-majorities. This way we stay together in the one church but respect the deep differences that exist among us.

TRADITIONALIST   An interesting suggestion indeed but

11

we have seen this movie before and I have an immediate observation. I note you are all for majorities at the Annual Conference and local church level. However, you are not at all for the majorities who have already spoken for over forty years in the highest council of our church, the General Conference. In other words, you want folk in Annual Conferences and local churches to respect and abide by the relevant majorities but you yourself are now prepared to set aside the majority decision that already exists. There is a fatal incoherence at the heart of your proposal when we begin to look at the fine print. You are already setting the platform for minorities down the line to ignore majority decisions when it suits them. So there is also a serious practical problem looming on the horizon that you are conveniently ignoring.

RECONCILER   To be honest, I had not noticed this problem until you mentioned it. However, I think you are misreading the actual effect of what I am proposing. I am not asking that we set aside the majority decisions we already have. I am asking for a fresh vote that would be taken by General Conference and it would only go into operation were it to be adopted by General Conference. I am working within our rules not against them.

TRADITIONALIST   Why are you even proposing this in the first place? You are naïve if you fail to see the problem you will cause for the evangelical side of the church. They cannot in good conscience live with your local option. Surely you know this already. Giving permission is granting legitimacy. If not naïve then you really are a progressive and this is a clever way to change the discipline of the church without fessing up to the radical character of your actions. You are introducing your progressive agenda by stealth and stages.

EVANGELICAL   Let me speak for myself here. I do not disagree with Traditionalist but I want to be heard on my own terms. This plan will indeed change the teaching of the church for it will reject the current teaching we actually hold and propose a local option that will make it abundantly clear that crucial units of The United Methodist Church actually endorse same-sex marriage and the ordination of practicing homosexuals. It sends a hopelessly confused mixed message, something we have long opposed. Pretending that this is not the case by saying that General Conference permits this state of affairs is a fudge. This is not how it will be read by most of our members and by the culture at large. It will be trumpeted as a full-scale victory. We will then witness either a massive exodus or a slow withdrawal of hosts of our people across the country.

RECONCILER   I understand this worry but don't you agree that this is one of those grey areas where thinking in black and white is mistaken. We both read and love the same Bible but we come away with different interpretations of its teaching. There is room for diversity here just as there is for pacifists and folk who believe in just war. In fact I am taking my stand with the Bible here; if the Bible fudges, to use your pejorative language, then let's be biblical; we should fudge too. I would prefer to explain it this way. If scripture does not really prohibit same-sex marriage then neither should we as United Methodists.

TRADITIONALIST   I know you would love to take us back into that merry-go-round again but I am not buying it. For Evangelical the issue is really as much about divine revelation as it is about scripture and I am tempted to think that at the end of the day you really have an incompetent deity lurking in your study. On a really depressing day I might even believe that when it comes to such an important issue before the church you are a functional atheist when God is not up to the job of getting through to us. I know this will shock you because you will protest that you love your Bible and preach consistently from it. But look again at the fine print. You have your own way of rerunning the arguments made twenty years ago by progressives. Let's face it you are now a progressive evangelical who has gone over to the other side. I admire your rhetorical brilliance and your ability to teach; I hope your royalties continue to roll in; but biblical scholarship is all over the map and it systematically ignores the crucial place of divine revelation in sorting through what to believe. In fact the way you speak of divine inspiration and divine speaking is a fine piece of theological obscurantism that could do with some analytical revisiting. Check out the way in which you switch from the language of inspiration to the language of divine speaking without noticing the cost implied.

EVANGELICAL   There you go again speaking for me without my permission. I spent a lot of money on my theological education and I wish you would butt out and let me continue where I left off. And I am getting tired of your hectoring tone. I have already said my piece about what to do with disagreement in interpreting scripture. We do our work and make a decision and we then let our conscience be bound by the Infallible Word of God. Of course, there is interpretation; who could ever deny this. But you make up your mind and then stand by what the Lord teaches us in scripture. So let's move on. I have two other big points I want to make to Reconciler. First, you have gone Baptist on us by proposing a congregational polity. We have enough problems with former Baptists as it stands without making things worse. I know they are good tithers and heaven knows we need them because of that; but deep down they want to put the local leaders totally in charge of local churches and they are skeptical about infant baptism. My objection is that you are at one stroke destroying the connectional polity of our church. And by doing that you have left the Methodist fold whatever else you may say about your loyalty to this or that slogan. Second...

RECONCILER   Now that is a low blow if ever I saw one.....I have been called many things recently but Baptist is a bit much. I have given my life to United Methodism and deserve a better reading than this; surely....

EVANGELICAL   Would you prefer a more irenic description of your position? Let me try again. We have been a connectional church from the beginning. With all its defects this polity has served us well and if time permitted I would make the case theologically for it. You are moving us towards a Congregational vision of Methodism that shreds our polity in the name of peace. And now let me make my second point. Your variation on the local option will not end the wars. It will now extend the fiasco we had in Tampa down into our Annual Conferences and into our local churches. It will absolutely tear us apart. This scheme of yours is dead on arrival; it is not a solution to the problem you yourself want to solve. You saw yourself what happened at General Conference; do you really want to replicate it at Annual Conferences and in local churches?

TRADITIONALIST   Can I add a point here?

RECONCILER   Go ahead, I am listening.

TRADITIONALIST   I am delighted to hear my evangelical friend speak up on behalf of our polity and ecclesial identity. I see an additional network of problems. Your proposal rewards disobedience and agitation. You make it in part because you want to end the conflict; but there are good and bad ways of ending conflict. This is not a good way for it sends a clear message that grandstanding and agitation really gets results. In addition, you seem to think that the non-heterosexual community will buy the analogy with heterosexual marriage in the long-haul. This is a total pipe-dream. How many genders do you acknowledge? I heard recently that on Facebook there are as many as fifty-two available. Even if we cut that down to five or so, what do you plan to propose as the relevant formal arrangements for bisexuals? Threesomes? Furthermore, have you kept up with the gay liberation literature on homosexual behavior? You are totally naive if you think that the homosexual community is going to stick with some version of the traditional conception of marriage. I could go deeper here and quote Hume when he said that reason is and always has been the slave of the passions. Neither modernity nor post modernity has any real brake on what is emerging once we allow our passions to dictate our morality. The Enlightenment was a fraud in what it promised. It promised a land of sweet order and reason and we have ended up with sensuality driving the moral bus over the cliff. Mark my words, and start by checking out the sociological developments among the young people of post-Christian Europe.

RECONCILER   If you keep this up I may well have to team up with the Evangelical to find a way forward. I really think I can win them over but if they break in your direction then the political prospects will look bleak. Let's start from the bottom of this barrage of objections and work back up to the top. I have no time for some kind of facile accommodation with the current culture of unbelief. I am an orthodox Christian who believes in the Trinity, in miracles, in Jesus, and in the Holy Spirit. I agree we have our hands full dealing with the intellectual questions we have to face. That's my first point. Second, I take exception to your description of the situation in the Christian homosexual community. These are good people who want to play their role in the life and leadership of the church. They have as much right to sexual satisfaction as heterosexuals do. The biblical texts do not address them as we now find them; they address situations where rape and violence were the relevant contexts; so we are facing something that is wholly new. I agree that what I am proposing does begin with taking conventional forms of marriage as the norm. This shows that I am not proposing that just anything goes. We should hold homosexuals to the same standard as heterosexuals, that is, chastity and fidelity. This will mean standing against the cultural currents if they are indeed as you describe. All we are doing is opening up a pathway to loyalty and love that is currently denied a minority that we have vilified and oppressed. You are right to the extent that there is unfinished business on the range of sexual identity but we can cross that bridge when we come to it with the ample resources of grace and love. As to rewarding agitation, bullying, and the like, I have absolutely no time for that. I am committed to dialogue and conferencing as much as you are. I hate this kind of behavior because it gets everybody worked up and we cannot get our own work done. So I stand by my track record. Others may want to reward bad ways of ending conflict; on this score I unapologetically plead not guilty.

TRADITIONALIST   So you really are opening up a Pandora's Box of options in sexual morality and you are asking us to trust you in advance like secular politicians do. Can't you see the long-term consequences of this decision?

PIETIST   Do you mind if we take a break at this point?

16

Dialogue II

A Surprising Dilemma for Progressive

PROGRESSIVE   I am so glad that we took a break. It interrupted the scare mongering that we were about to witness and gives us a fresh chance to listen to what Reconciler is trying to get us to hear. Frankly, I was taken aback when I read the splendid articulation of his views. It came as a bolt from the blue. I have long admired him for his extraordinary work in the local church. Evangelicals seem to have a lock on church planting and growth. Yet deep down I generally feel that I cannot trust the evangelicals. They are really the Tea Party within our church; they want to take it over and make it an outpost of the Republican Party. So I was not just cautious but skeptical. Now I feel so much better for it is clear that Reconciler has come clean and adopted a crucial element in the progressive agenda. This is really good news. Come to think of it, we already designate local churches in our camp as Reconciling Churches! Welcome home!

EVANGELICAL   Good news for you and very bad news for us!

PROGRESSIVE   Let me see if I can take the measure of this rapidly changing situation. Our side faces a dilemma at this point. On the one hand, the proposal before us is a great first step. Many of us can accept the local option, for it at long last gives us the freedom to exercise the ministry we long ago adopted. As the old saying goes, half a loaf is better than no bread. On the other hand, we would still be part of a church where the default position goes against us, where there would be a host of local units that are still free to pursue their bigotry and oppression at will. Do I really want to be a part of a church which condones such bigotry and oppression? No. Absolutely no! Can you imagine us taking this line on slavery, segregation, racism, or women's ordination? No. We are really all in on the ending of discrimination and inclusion

17

or we are not. This is a matter of justice and equality and you cannot get off this train once you get on board. To this extent I have sympathy with the more conservative wing of the evangelical party; it is hard to see how we can keep them on board once we take this turn in the road. I suppose that in the short term I can go along and vote for this proposal but to be honest this will not bring our campaign to a halt. Our differences will revolve around tactics rather than the ultimate goal we are determined to reach. Some will totally reject the move by Reconciler to divide us into three units; this would be a totally unacceptable compromise of principle. We will have to live with this potential division as best we can.

TRADITIONALIST   There we go again unfurling the banner of your unstoppable ideology. Have you and your friends ever thought through what would happen if you were really in charge either of United Methodism or your own Progressive United Methodism? How would you have won the day or come into existence? Surely, it would be by the systematic undermining over the years of our order and discipline. Now what do you think is going to happen when the first big hurricane comes through your new town? You will have so undermined the whole idea of discipline and canon law that any regulations you have in place will go up in smoke. It will be like what happened when that seminary up in Denver taught courses on subverting corrupt systems from within and then witnessed the students turn around and use what they learned against the faculty. I love the ironic justice when this kind of thing happens. I predict that you will be fine for a generation or two at the most; then just watch how your own weapons will be turned against you when folk want to adopt whatever is the latest fad in theology and ethics.

PROGRESSIVE   Actually this does not bother us in the least, for we do not share your legalistic mind-set. Why do you think we worked to have the practice of just resolution put in the *Book of Discipline*? We need to move to a much more therapeutic vision of conflict resolution rather than always reaching for the rule book and throwing it at people. Have you never heard of grace and redemption? We operate with a totally difference conception of church order than you do. We are looking to implement a much more grace-filled way of dealing with conflict. We have had our fill of trials. The money and energy thus saved will be directed to taking care of the marginalized and poor in our neighborhoods.

TRADITIONALIST   I wish you well in your endeavors. They are a will-of-the-wisp that does not begin to reckon with the wild human intellect and with the wayward passions of even the elect of God you claim to represent. Canon law is not the nasty institution you think it is. Think of the secular analogy. I assume you are opposed to the abuse of women and children by adults. Law is there initially to express the judgment of a people that this kind of behavior is unacceptable; it will not be tolerated. So its first function is expressive. Suppose we have a law against abuse on the books. If judges and officers of the court decided to ignore the law, their action would undermine the expressive judgments of the people concerned. Of course, it would also leave folk unprotected but that is another aspect of law we need not take up here. So I can understand why you engage in the practice of jury nullification, law nullification, and the like, in the courts of the church. You cleverly and systematically set out to undermine the expressive function of law and to undermine the official teaching of the church from within. Dressing all this up in terms of just resolution fools only those who are not thinking things through to the bottom. It will all come back to bite you down the road when your spiritual children deploy the same tactics against your progressive agenda. And by way of a footnote, it really is a joke that you play your therapeutic cards on one day of the week and then plan ugly demonstrations the next!

PROGRESSIVE   You are trying to trap me with your fancy footwork but I am not going to be fooled. One thing we know and understand: Our church is wrong in its speech and action towards the LGBITQ community. We will use every avenue open to us to change the church and bring it to repentance. We will work the therapeutic angle when it is appropriate and we will also plan demonstrations to move things forward. We are not giving up our God-given vocation to act prophetically and effectively.

EVANGELICAL   So we can expect the same chaos we experienced at the last General Conference in 2016 in Portland?

PROGRESSIVE   Yes. Our friends in the civic community in Portland are delighted we are coming because they can make this another national Rainbow event given the press interest in the current crisis within United Methodism. They have already told us how elated they are; and we are working on the contacts already in place. Of course, we will need to coordinate our efforts with the presiding bishops but that is not a problem given the members who now publicly support our position. Maybe we will have to tone things down a bit, but I predict significant action to get our church to move forward in the light of the new insights given to us in the last generation.

Standing Firm in the Ethos of United Methodist Assemblies

TRADITIONALIST   This is an unsurprising revelation. I expected as much when I heard that we were moving to Portland; even the meeting place of General Conference is now a political undertaking. So let me make a proposal. Let's ask the Commission on General Conference to send an immediate telegram indicating that we are rescinding our plans to have Portland host our General Conference. Every which way we turn we are being led like a lamb to the slaughter. Of course, there will be much wailing and gnashing of teeth in response. We will be told that the contracts have been signed and we cannot back out. Don't we have any smart lawyers who can challenge any action taken against us? It is time we stopped this guerilla war and tried to move to more neutral territory. We need to take a stand right from the start and follow up all down the line at this point if we are to survive as a church with any kind of order and integrity. If that fails then we close off General Conference from the general public and call the police to stop any demonstrations that the progressives may seek to deploy.

EVANGELICAL   Calm down my friend. Don't call the lawyers or police just yet. If we can get the right plan for separation a rally like the one anticipated in Portland could work in our favor. It would reveal the depths of the divisions that already exist and cause enough pain for folk to see the real merit in what we are currently discussing as one option among many.

TRADITIONALIST   Are your discussing separation or planning for separation? There is a real difference, you know. Which is it?

EVANGELICAL   Both! Not everyone in our camp is fully signed on to separation despite what you read and hear. We are not stupid. We will discuss all the options open to us. And that will entail that we look specifically at the option of separation. Will anyone else even open their minds, much less their hearts and doors to all the options if we do not tackle this elephant in the room? As I say, we are not stupid; if we did not go to the right schools we met the scholars coming home. If anything is to get through there will have to be a broad coalition of conservative evangelicals, centrists, sacramentalists, orthodox, charismatics, and institutionalists. It is hard to keep the different groups straight, but we need a broad coalition. We will look at all the options that we think might work to preserve the riches of the Wesleyan and Methodist tradition. We are not going to hang around wringing our hands like our friends in the other mainline churches did. We have done our homework and talked with them at length. They tell us they made two fatal mistakes. They failed to see how fast things would develop; and they were not together. We will not make those mistakes.

TRADITIONALIST   Have you thought of mounting a counter-demonstration? How about getting a New Orleans marching jazz band to troop through the tables of General Conference with a coffin at the head of it marked, "The Death of United Methodism"? Maybe they should play "When the Saints Go Marching in." Better still; let's have one of those magnificent funeral dirges to send a clear message to the world at large. That would teach that dysfunctional council of bishops a lesson. Think of the scrambling we would witness behind the podium. It would put them in the same bind that emerged when the Confessing Movement tried to sign up local churches to their cause and have them identify as Confessing Churches. They immediately made it illegal to do this kind of thing. But, of course, no action was taken against the Reconciling Communities folk. Maybe you should join the club and get up a counter-demonstration! I am sure you can find the money to hire one of those wonderful marching bands!

EVANGELICAL I take it that you are pulling my leg at this point. I am glad that you have begun to calm down and recover your old curmudgeonly self! We all need to lighten up a bit. Seriously, this has never been an option. We are not going to play that game. It will not work for our people. It would mean we would lose the high moral ground in defense of our polity. And it would give our opponents an opportunity to demonize us afresh.

PROGRESSIVE I really wish you evangelicals would stop playing the victim. You are a bunch of white males with a set of docile, token females in tow who have been oppressing the rest of use for long enough. We have had enough of your whining and your efforts to run away from reality. Can't you see who the real victims are here? We are not playing games when we demonstrate. We are standing up for the oppressed and will not stop until our church repents of its harmful ways of speaking and acting. The problem is not homosexuality it is homophobia. We are tired watching conservatives making the institution the priority rather than the people it has harmed across the years.

Contested Divine Intervention

PIETIST Can I say a word at this point? I have been quietly praying throughout our planned dialogue session and I think I am now ready to speak. In fact I spent Lent of this year listening to the Holy Spirit and grieving over the state of our church. I am so glad to see that we are seated around a round table. You know E. Stanley Jones took this from his friends in India and I have come to see that it may be the way forward for all of us. Jones is one of my heroes so you will probably find echoes of his work in what I will try to say. However, I speak for myself here. Or rather I want to share what the Holy Spirit has been telling me over these last several months. I have been spending a lot of time

22

listening to the Inner Voice.

PROGRESSIVE   Now that is interesting because one of the finest bishops of our church spoke in a similar manner at the Connectional Table recently. She said the Holy Spirit had told her to propose to the Connectional Table that we should change our language on homosexuality at the next General Conference and the proposal was passed. This language and imagery of table seems to have caught on over the last few years. I really like the associations the language of tables brings to the table, if I may overuse the term. It gets us away from the language of debates, and votes, and trials, and those harsh hierarchical ways of thinking and acting.

PIETIST   Now isn't that a coincidence! Or should I say wonderful providence? I too have been convicted that our thinking is much too hierarchical and dualistic where one side has to win against another side and really everyone ends up a loser. I have to make a confession at this point. I used to be part of that whole way of thinking. I was on the conservative side all my life and readily joined in the guerilla war we were waging. I thought in terms of them and us, of winners and losers, of the superior and the inferior. I gladly joined in working from the worst caricature of my opponents. The Holy Spirit convicted me that this was wrong. I have been in great sorrow and anguish since then about the terrible harm we are doing to the church, the bride of Christ.

TRADITIONALIST   Before we get too carried away here, can I get clear on what I am hearing. Are you folk, I mean, you two, Progressive and Pietist, are you seriously claiming that you have a new divine revelation on your hands? I have a faint memory that a bishop took this line maybe twenty years ago but her claim faded away rather quietly. I think her name was Bishop Judith Craig and she announced the revelation in the Episcopal Address. I could tell it was a deeply pious moment for a lot of folk; though many had no idea what was really going on.

PROGRESSIVE   To be honest this kind of talk makes me nervous. I am just reporting what happened at this point; I am not to the point of endorsing it.

PIETIST   Now hear me out here; I know it is difficult. Yes. I am saying that the Holy Spirit spoke to me and inspired me to share this message not just with my beloved United Methodism but with other groups that are facing the same challenge we are.

EVANGELICAL   I hear echoes of Reconciler's views on divine inspiration in what you say. Insofar as I understand his theology, Reconciler really wants to say that we are subject to the same inspiration that the biblical authors experienced. We are not prepared to swallow that pill. We do not stand in the same place as the prophets, evangelists, and apostles. He mixes up the language of inspiration with language about divine speaking. Come to think of it, parts of it sound like a reiteration of the language of dictation that Reconciler elsewhere rejects. After all divine dictation is just a species of divine speaking. This sort of talk is confusing and misleading. We could pursue this further but let me cut to the quick. What is on offer from Pietist is a claim to have a fresh Word from God for today. If that is the case are we now adding new material to the divine revelation given in the Bible? Now I am not just getting nervous; I am aggressively opposed to any such move. Are you saying that we should open up the canon and add this new Word to scripture?

PIETIST   Honestly, I would never go that far for I am generally conservative in my approach to scripture. I am not too sure how to put all this together, so bear with me. Let me cut to the chase and tell you what I feel the Holy Spirit told me. First, we really must stop oppressing our homosexual brothers and sisters. Second, there is room for another interpretation of all those negative texts on homosexuality in the Bible. Third, we really should consider changing our discipline to reflect the law of love for God and neighbor. We are a people who believe in grace and it is time we took the radical implications of love and grace in meeting the genuine concerns of our homosexual friends, children, and neighbors. Fourth, the way forward is then to gather round a round table and listen to each other and pray that God will show us all a way forward.

EVANGELICAL   I thought that you were on our side in this debate. Like Reconciler you have gone and joined the progressives!

24

I am absolutely dumb-founded; I can scarcely find words…

PIETIST   Now hold on a minute. Please do not dish out the kind of venom that I learned to hand out to our opponents before I went through this radical transformative experience with the Holy Spirit. I have talked this over with numerous people and they are beginning to see my point. We have been far too judgmental in our attitudes and far too uptight in our dogmatic systems of conservative theology. Brother Stanley was right to say that all we really needed was the affirmation that Jesus was Lord. The rest we can leave open as we seek to follow the mind of the Spirit.

EVANGELICAL   I am tempted to think that maybe there is something to the story that evangelicals have a more serious problem with defection than I realized. And to think that I looked up to you as one of our best leaders who was trained in Wesley Studies and who could lead us in the renewal of our church. Clearly, I have some more thinking to do when we are finished here.

PIETIST   All I can tell you is that I have prayed about this whole matter and this is what the Lord told me. I am not saying that I am infallible. All I am asking is that we bring folk together around a round table and hear one another with an intensity that we have never done before. We can then trust the Lord to find a way through to a better future. Indeed I am encouraged to know that one of our most spiritually minded bishops agrees with me on this. He has suggested we stop the propaganda, declare a moratorium on the celebrations and trials regarding same gender-unions, and begin a practice of prayer and discernment that leaves our preferences at the door as we enter this extended period of seeking only God's direction. Can't you see that God may want the United Methodists to do a new thing? Can't you hear what the Spirit seems to be saying to the church today?

TRADITIONALIST   I hope you are not implying that the rest of us have not been praying about this issue as well. I am not as schooled in the highways and byways of spiritually as you are, but I have my own modest ways of seeking the will of God. I have to tell you that God has told me nothing of the kind over all the years I have been seeking his guidance. Now it is an elementary first step in Christian theology that we are called to test the spirits. Maybe you think that this is dualistic or hierarchical or any one of a number of intellectual vices that you think we mortals are prone to in this strange world God has given us. However, my first test is that anyone who professes to hear a Word from God that improves on our Lord's teaching on marriage is not going to get to first base. So count me out from either taking you seriously or sitting around your table until we get a fresh Word from God. Let me be blunt. Where did you get this account of divine revelation? Is this what evangelicals now believe? Have you become so confused on the first principles of divine revelation that you fall for this kind of pious nonsense?

PIETIST   I know all this is hard to swallow but there it is. I can only share what I am convinced that the Holy Spirit has led me to think after a period of intense repentance and soul-searching.

TRADITIONALIST   And I can only reiterate that I most respectfully think that you are profoundly mistaken. Let me add another point. If I cannot convince you that your account of the criteria for personal divine revelation has not been thought through, let me try a little old-fashioned logic. You know that Wesley was a stickler for logic and reason; so grant me at the outset that you will give me a hearing on this front.

Logic and Reason at the Round Table

PIETIST   You are indeed right about Mr. Wesley; and even the beginning student in Wesley Studies will agree with what you just said.

TRADITIONALIST   Let me get clear on what is at issue. On the one hand, you are offering a Word from the Holy Spirit. I confess you are not always as clear as you might be on this point but I can only go on a plain reading of your position. If this is truly a Word from the Holy Spirit not just for you but for the church, then we are intellectually obliged to believe it and act on it. If God said it, that settles it, we should believe it. I take it that this is Logic 101 on divine revelation. If I remember correctly, Wesley's mother taught him this lesson early in his career.

PIETIST   I agree with your premises and your conclusions. This is one reason why my own life has gone through something of a serious upheaval of late. Both logic and (I would add) loyalty to God require that I believe and obey what I have heard from the Holy Spirit. I suppose there is an analogue here with the call of the Holy Spirit to ordained ministry.

TRADITIONALIST   Now here is the problem. In agreeing with the noble and pious bishop you are recommending that we all come to these wonderful polished round tables, presumably set up by the Commission on General Conference, and leave our preferences at the door. Can you see the conflict here? You will come with your divinely inspired preference for same-sex marriage and all that this implies. Are you now going to hide these beliefs under the table or under your chair or in your back-pocket? You have told us you have to believe and obey what God has told you. So there is no question of your being able to leave them at the door. So either you have to take your new Word from the Holy Spirit as genuine and keep it with you at your spot on the table or you must reinterpret it as a preference that has no standing in the debate and that should therefore be left at the door. I suppose you might accuse me of dualistic thinking at this point. I prefer to stand with the good old Methodist tradition of common sense and sound reasoning instead.

EVANGELICAL   I really like the way Traditionalist is hitting the nail on the head here. Note please that I am using metaphor; I have no hammer and nails hidden under my end of the table. But I would prefer to take a more modest line at this stage. Let's get real here and recognize what is happening. This is one more effort to resolve our disputes by discernment, dialogue, and holy conferencing. I am done with these. Two points should make clear why. First, our church has been conferencing on the relevant issues for forty years and the verdict is in. We have a gracious and defensible position and it is time we moved on. We have a process; it is not perfect; but the process has run its course and it is too late now to start from scratch. Indeed, starting from scratch is a way of being in deep denial about the legitimacy of the outcomes of our long and tangled deliberative procedures. Second, we now know what this sort of thing involves. It is an effort to wear down the opposition and bring us to heel. I will no longer be complicit in this kind of self-delusional activity. This is one more effort to keep the debate going and pretend that our church has not taken a principled stance that should be respected in its content and upheld in practice.

TRADITIONALIST   I sense that my evangelical friend is beginning to get the picture and get some backbone. Stay the course and we may yet get agreement on what to do. Before we move on, notice that Pietist has introduced another common conviction that can readily get overlooked. Am I right, Pietist, that you really think all we need for the content of church doctrine is that three-word summary that made the rounds in ecumenical circles in the twentieth century, namely, "Jesus is Lord"?

PIETIST   I fear that you are loading your dualistic gun and getting ready to take aim and use it on me again. Let me beat you to the draw this time. No doubt you will tell me that this is something far short of Nicene Orthodoxy and even further away from the expansion of doctrine we have in our Articles of Religion and Confession of Faith. Indeed it is! The simple confession that Jesus is Lord fits much better with the overall teaching of the New Testament as a summary of faith. Maybe I should have said that this is where we should at least start. It is where many Boards of Ordained Ministry now start. But I am getting off course. Let me put my point another way, a way that may be attractive to my friend, Reconciler. Leave aside my change of mind on sexual morality. Think of the issue this way. Surely the only kind of issues that we should treat as church-dividing are those that fall into the domain of orthodox doctrine. We should not divide over moral issues. To put the matter in the language of scholarship, we should not make moral issues a matter of *status confessionis*.

The Status of Division over Morality

EVANGELICAL   I like the Latin touch; I wish I had your way with words. This is a very good question. It keeps cropping up on the edges of my network and I am a loss at how to answer it. I have even given some attention to it myself on and off. One of my bishop friends finds this a very compelling argument and has put it to me on several occasions. I think when push comes to shove he would go with the conservative side of the church but he is clearly hesitating.

TRADITIONALIST   Your compromising underwear is beginning to show again, my friend! Take it to the theological laundry and see what happens.

EVANGELICAL   Actually, I did this the last day after I talked with my bishop friend and here are my thoughts. For starters, we are a holiness tradition. It is surely strange that the pietists in the one tradition in modern Christianity that bet the store on holiness now want to relegate morality to an entirely secondary status and lift up orthodoxy as the backbone of the church. I am all for orthodoxy and our doctrinal standards but think of what is going on here. We get everyone worked up about the legitimacy of anal sex and other kinds of sexual practice that we dare not mention in public. We then ask the church to allow one party to endorse it while the rest of us permit it. Permission is of course simply a euphemism for legitimizing. We then claim that they are really secondary issues that should under no circumstances be allowed to divide us. It is only if the General Conference tampers with something like the Trinity or the resurrection that should prompt debate about potential division. As I said earlier, most days of the week I see no way to solve our dilemma other than by division, but now that you raise the issue explicitly I have to deal with it.

PROGRESSIVE   Can I remind you all that Wesley has some very negative things to say about orthodoxy? For my part I have no interest in returning to some sort of dogmatic orthodoxy and starting up heresy trials; I never really believed the orthodox version of Christianity. I have long believed that the heart of our tradition focuses on transformation not doctrine. We are not a doctrinal church; we are a church of grace and compassion. Besides, I was schooled to think for myself and to develop a truly contemporary interpretation of the Christian message.

EVANGELICAL   Hold that thought for a moment till I try and sort through what Pietist is suggesting. Recall that the claim I am nervously trying to weigh is that we should only consider division when orthodox doctrine is at stake. I am not very good at this but I had a philosophy class in seminary and I picked up a common way to sort out what is at stake; it may work here. Let's do a little thought experiment. Suppose one of the smaller churches in Utah made a petition to the General Conference asking that The United Methodist Church permit polygamy. Suppose further that there was a coalition of North American delegates made up of those who were sympathetic to freedom of religion for conservative Mormons and of a network of well-organized delegates from outside the United States. Suppose this group managed to get a majority vote in the General Conference. Do you think that this should be treated as church-dividing? I know I am beginning to look foolish here, but now that I have started let me become even more foolish. Suppose our church endorsed a whole raft of moral evils, like discrimination against women, the use of potentially lethal torture for terrorists, rape in times of war, polyandry for an obscure United Methodist tribe in some faraway forest, and torturing babies alive at three o'clock in the morning for fun? Forgive me for being so worked up here and for even mentioning such evils. I am merely trying to make a point. It would be a strange soul who would say that this should not be considered as potentially church-dividing. Any one of them would send shock-waves through the system; and folk would argue that those who introduced this were tearing the church apart. Many would leave and form another denomination and rightly so. It is not at all difficult to think of a moral practice that would justifiably become church-dividing. If this holds, then the whole effort to claim that division should only occur if orthodox doctrine was overturned in the courts of our church falls apart. And those who would be standing for the truth would not be the church-dividers; it is those who introduce alien moral teaching and practice who would be dividing the church.

TRADITIONALIST   You surprise me, Evangelical, by the dexterity of your reply. Even so, I thought you would have been far more biblical at this point.

EVANGELICAL   What do you mean? Does scripture speak to this issue?

TRADITIONALIST   Don't you remember Paul's dramatic action in handing over the fellow who was sleeping with his father's wife? And what about that text where Jesus makes it clear that it were better we had a millstone put round our necks and cast into the sea than we cause one of his little ones to stumble? And what about those texts of Jesus that make moral action the very criterion of approval at the last judgment? It is hard to read these texts (and many more I could cite) and then conclude that moral proposals should be treated as secondary in the teaching of the church.

The Three Buckets Method

RECONCILER   Not so fast, Traditionalist. Before we proceed we need to employ my three bucket test. I think we should put these texts in the bucket that contains all those verses which should be interpreted as fitting to the original context but no longer fit for moral purposes today. They do not reflect the timeless will of God nor are they categorically wrong; they are relative to the time in which they were spoken. So you see there is a third way here to consider; stop thinking merely in terms of black and white.

TRADITIONALIST   I am so glad you brought up these wonderful buckets of yours. Tell me this: Did you get these three buckets from the Bible or did you find these down at the hardware store? I have been looking all over the place for them in the scriptures and so far have failed to find them. So, I can only conclude that you got them at Home Depot. Remarkably, I could not find them there when I asked at the information desk. Did you design and invent these buckets yourself? They are certainly not biblical but

31

extra-biblical. The effort then, to unravel my counter-argument and lay claim to being more biblical-than-thou fails to persuade.

PIETIST There you go again with your logic-chopping, your militant attitude, and your dualistic thinking. Can't you exercise some charity and take the wider point that there will be legitimate differences of interpretation about how to understand and apply these texts today? Reconciler was simply using a useful image to get our attention; we all know the real point he is making. Scripture leaves these things open to be worked out at the round table of prayer and discernment. This is the way they worked things out in the first councils of the church. Once we grant this, then we are free to follow scripture in a less dogmatic and more loving way. We can see the big picture for what it is and from that angle we can then pick out the shadows and dark spots that operate to show the light that scripture really gives us. It is akin to what many folk claim when they say we would never really understand what goodness is if there were no evil in the world.

Weighing Gains and Losses

PROGRESSIVE This whole conversation brings me back to my original dilemma: Should I welcome Reconciler and Pietist into my camp and work towards a coalition with them? Or should I keep them at a distance because they really represent a fifth column that will drag me back into a world of orthodoxy and Biblicism that would threaten the wider elements in my progressive agenda? I really like Reconciler for the most part but I have to say that Pietist's flowery language and tone make me cringe. I am stuck between a rock and a hard place, as they say. I want to make a tactical alliance with Reconciler and Pietist and move things forward but I worry about the theological baggage that they bring to the table. I also worry that deep down I am perhaps betraying my own principles.

EVANGELICAL I understand this kind of dissonance. We face the same kind of dilemma when we try to count the votes and see what we can realistically achieve. We recognize that we have to have the votes if we are to get anything done. However, I am surprised that you dwell on it. Reconciler surely gives you all that your heart ultimately desires. On his proposal there will be a full-scale, legitimate, progressive wing of the church in which you can implement your agenda. We long ago realized that the church had lost its bearings on sound doctrine but there was little we could do about it other than form renewal groups to try and get straight on the historical record and get the church to take more seriously her constitutional standards of doctrine. This was to be a cross-generational effort and we were prepared to be patient. We have had limited but real success here. Many of the folk whose theological education we funded at the doctoral level have done great work even though we have had a fair number who took our money and made peace with the enemy. The pressure to conform was too much for them. Happily, we have won more than we've lost on this bet. On the positive front, I have it on good authority that Albert Outler changed his mind in the last years of his life on his railing against orthodoxy, on pluralism, on the Statement on our Theological Task, and even on the quadrilateral. However, the church lives off the memory of the Outler of popular faith and not the real Outler of history so this does not help us in our current crisis. I would have thought Progressive, that you would have called in the band for a celebration given what Reconciler offers you. You can bank what is being handed out and go right back to work to finish the job. Given the defeats you have suffered across the years, I would have thought you would be thrilled at what has transpired of late. Some of your opponents scored a home goal. It would not be difficult to write a road-map on how to proceed to harass the conservative wing of the church and make life so difficult that they will have to leave. This will then let you pick up the property, the public relations victory for your cause, and all the other assets.

RECONCILER   Leaving aside your pejorative sentences, you can do the same in your section of the church for you will have the option of forming your own conservative wing of the denomination. Those in the middle can be designated as discerning, undecided, and agnostic or whatever works for them. So surely you can see merit in my proposed third way. Nobody can get all that they desire; my plan gives you all the room you really need given your convictions.

EVANGELICAL   Not at all. I am not going to rehearse my earlier points about the cost involved, not least the cost of turning us into something akin to a Congregational denomination. I know you mean well and that you have thought long and hard about the issues. However, you really do not understand how deep the issues run for us. People think that we are obsessed with sex when it is the progressives who have insisted of making this an issue for the whole church. Frankly, sexual morality is simply the presenting issue. The real issue is biblical authority and divine revelation. You are asking us to accept or to condone behavior that we are convinced is sinful because it is contrary to the Word of God. Of course, we also stand for sound orthodox doctrine, because we think it too is biblical. As you know, we are also concerned about the decline of the church in North America. This too we think is linked to biblical authority and sound doctrine. Frankly, I do not think we can hold our people in place much longer. Up until now we have been able to say to them that we stand for the official stance of the church and that the progressives are out of line with its teaching and practice. They refuse to abide by these and are moving hell and high-water to impose their views on the whole church. So there is a stark missionary dilemma for us. We have a disastrous public relations problem that gets worse by the month. Consider that not a single bishop has ever resolutely acknowledged in public either the difficulty we face or the service we have rendered. At best they operate with a vision of moral equivalence: those who uphold the practice and teaching of the church are on equal footing with those who are systematically undermining it. At worst they think we are the real troublers of Israel and should either behave ourselves or go home to the backwoods of Kentucky where we belong. Forgive me for going on at such length here but you must acknowledge that the cards are stacked against us and it is very hard to get our full message across. Maybe this is the reason why your bridge across the extremes only reaches one side of the river. You are all for reconciling with progressive; you are not really interested in reaching out to our side in the debate.

RECONCILER   You last point cannot be quite right; I am here talking with you face to face right now. More importantly, I think you misread the missionary situation. We are shooting ourselves in the foot with the new generation that is coming through, including the new generation of clergy. I know what it takes to grow a church, my record is the best in the denomination, and I am willing to bet the store that we will make it through and be able to grow the three distinct kinds of churches I am proposing.

EVANGELICAL   No-one is challenging your success in church growth. I have been to your conferences and they are terrific. Your success happened, however, before you changed your mind and went public. No doubt you have the skill to walk your church through to your Congregational polity, so you will be fine. But the jury is at best out on the big picture and the evidence from other churches that took your position does not tell in your favor. Besides, this debate cannot be settled by mere appeal to cultural trends or numerical success, as you yourself acknowledge. And given what Progressive is likely to say, there remains the horrendous problem of extending the chaos of General Conference down into our Annual Conferences and local churches.

Ecclesial Compatibilists and Incompatibilists

TRADITIONALIST   At the risk of being accused of acting picky and theologically exacting, surely there is also the matter of our vision of the church. Like it or not, we need to face up to a further choice that rarely gets mentioned. On the one side, there are those who think that we can agree to disagree and that both positions and their variations can be rightly accommodated within the one body. Let's call these folk *compatibilists*. On the other side, there are those who do not think you can accommodate the opposing positions within the one body. Let's call these folk *incompatibilists*. There is a real either/or here which cannot be fudged. I think my evangelical friend is really an incompatibilist for otherwise discussing and planning for separation does not make sense.

PROGRESSIVE   I hate the nasty, technical language you use here, but I get the point. I suppose in the short term I am a compatibilist as a matter of tactics; in the long run I am an incompatibilist as a matter of theological principle. Evangelical, for once, is right. We have no intention of accommodating to a church which harbors bigotry and practices oppression. As one of our more aggressive units insists, love will prevail. And so will justice and truth.

RECONCILER   I am not sure I like the language but I am clearly a compatibilist. And I think that once Progressive and her allies begin to experience the freedom they long for they will change their minds and live at peace.

PIETIST   That would be my hope too. Yet, I have to add that I think this way of thinking takes us right back to the dualistic, hierarchical way of thinking and acting that we should long ago have abandoned.

EVANGELICAL   Was that a segment of the divine guidance you received or did you get that part from one of the books in you library? Alright, I take that sarcastic question back. But one has to wonder!

TRADITIONALIST   If we let my distinction stand I think we can begin to see where folk are beginning to line up. Let's agree that Progressive, Reconciler, and Pietist are compatibilists. We can now expect that they will all work together for some sort of local option as the best way forward at the next General Conference. Now wouldn't you like to be a fly on the wall when that conversation begins to happen?

RECONCILER   I think that you are right on how things are going to fall out. You can rest assured that we are going to get our political act together across the connection and win at the next General Conference. I lost the vote at the last one but there is not going to be a repeat performance of the mistakes I made then. So I look forward to working with Progressive and Pietist to get things changed this next time around.

EVANGELICAL   Can't you see, Traditionalist, they are all progressives on the presenting issue. The other elements that bring out their differences are bells and whistles that are certainly interesting and even important but we need to face reality here and come clean on where they stand on marriage. This is a huge development that we ignore at our peril. The wedge issue is marriage and if lose on that the game is over. And of course, Progressive is only a tactical compatibilist but a compatibilist all the same. So it looks as if you and I are the only incompatibilists. So what are we going to do, Traditionalist? You oppose separation as you stated so abruptly at the beginning. At the very least I want to have it as an option on the table as we move forward. The stakes are too high for us not to have the nuclear option in order to preserve the treasures we have inherited across the years. It is a bit like papal infallibility for Roman Catholicism; we need it as a last resort. I do not want to be apocalyptic about our situation, but we cannot pretend that we do not need an exit strategy that will work for us. Maybe you and I should sit down on our own and explore our differences face to face.

TRADITIONALIST   That's fine by me.

RECONCILER   If that is the case why don't the rest of us do the same? Pietist, Progressive, and I are effectively on the same page on the need for the revision of our *Book of Discipline*, so perhaps we should spend some time on our own too.

PROGRESSIVE AND PIETIST   Let's do it.

Dialogue III

Differences between Traditionalist and Evangelical

TRADITIONALIST   Perhaps we are much closer than we realize. I agree that the fat is in the fire and we have to deal with it. Before I get to the specific proposals I favor, let me back off a minute. To be frank, I am disappointed in the lack of militancy that you display. I use the term 'militancy' deliberately. Maybe I have spent too much time with the Fighting Irish but this is not a time for pious slogans and lack of clarity on hard questions that have to be answered. We are being muzzled at every turn because we are constantly told to avoid extreme language and be nice to everybody. This is a recipe for evasion; it simply postpones the day of reckoning.

EVANGELICAL   Speaking of how we use terms, who are you anyway? I would have thought that a traditionalist is a species of conservatism and evangelicalism is a species of conservatism. So you are really one of us. Why muddy the waters further on us by splitting hairs?

TRADITIONALIST   Traditionalist is the person who stands first and foremost for the official stance of The United Methodist Church as expressed in our doctrines, discipline, and practices since we began life in 1968. She is tired of the destruction of our church from within by those who can no longer abide by what it is canonically. We could go into a whole sidebar on how this might be defended. Clearly there is significant overlap with any conservative who wants to conserve the riches of the tradition. But too many conservatives today in the political arena are not conservatives; they are radicals who want to tear things up by the roots and start all over from scratch. I need a space where I can set a more forceful tone, defend who we are officially even with all our faults, and stand up against the revisionists who show no quarter in the fight to turn us into something entirely new on the basis of worthless promissory notes. I really am militant in preserving the treasures of United Methodism, fragile and fallible though they are in places. This starts with a realistic assessment of the forces at work right now. If we continue down the road of the local option, for example, we will simply move from the present chaos, into fragmentation, and then to an unpleasant and speedy death. Of course, this is a historical judgment on my part but not to decide is to decide when you are standing in the flow of history. You have to follow the lights you have.

EVANGELICAL   Aren't you being a bit harsh here? As an evangelical I am just trying to be gracious and magnanimous. We are also trying to get beyond the stereotyping that has dogged our political efforts to date.

TRADITIONALIST   No matter what you do you are going to be demonized and cast in a bad light. You are already identified as the Gang of Eighty by those who claim to be peace-loving United Methodists who say in the same breath that they want to lower the rhetorical temperature! Folk are all over you for not releasing the names of the people involved and are charging you with lack of transparency. You are painted as a homophobic, power-hungry minority setting out to achieve the ultimate takeover of United Methodism. One of your folk, generally recognized as a senior scholar in Methodism, has been called out on Facebook as a Calvinist by a distinguished journalist in United Methodism now in retirement. His work was also blackballed by a leading progressive bishop in the higher echelons of the publishing house. His work never made it onto the list of materials to be used in United Methodist curriculum. His opponents care nothing about what he may have argued in print. Forget about winning the public relations war as your first step forward; you win that war in the end by standing on truth and principle. Your opponents will show no mercy. They will spread disinformation about their opponents in a heartbeat. They will accuse you of hating gay people. More subtly they will write blogs claiming that your church is not gay-friendly. They will work up strategies to make you guilty by association. They know exactly what innuendo to deploy; this comes so naturally they do not need to think about it. Of course, there are exceptions; we all know folk on the other side who are the salt of the earth and a paragon of courtesy. But you must see the big picture as well.

EVANGELICAL   I know. I know.

TRADITIONALIST   We are in the midst of a guerilla war where the stakes are the crown jewels of United Methodism and the extension of a theological and cultural revolution into the heart of the church. They are experienced operators and are relentless in pursuing their goals. So forget about how you will be received; you lost that round long ago, as your comments about the bishops makes only too clear.

EVANGELICAL   All this is strong medicine. I am not sure I want to even hear this. We want to take a more conciliatory line this time around.

TRADITIONALIST   Let me give you another possible scenario that has not been mentioned. Maybe this will awaken you to the depths of the crisis that we face. I am sure there are folk out there who would like nothing better than for you to pack up and leave. At best they tolerate you. They cringe whenever they have to deal with you; they stoically endure your stony silence when they introduce resolution after resolution banging away at their agenda at Annual Conference. They double down after defeat. They get a kick out of going to your free breakfasts at Annual Conference all decked out in their dress code. Outwardly they smile; inwardly they are there to spy out what you are planning and to make you feel uncomfortable in your own meetings. They will keep you out of the Districts they have managed to take over and be delighted when you are sent to faraway appointments. They simply put up with you as best they can. At worst they hate you and everything that you stand for. They would never admit this, of course. They love it when you make a mistake. They are bitterly disappointed when you make an inch of progress to strengthen the current teaching and practices of the church. You stand in their way. They would love to see you leave, even as they would not for a moment say anything like that in public.

41

EVANGELICAL   Perhaps this is a tad exaggerated; and I understand the tendency to be dramatic but let me agree for the moment.

TRADITIONALIST   Here is what some of them honestly believe behind closed doors. They are convinced that if they can bend the church's position in their direction, say, with some complicated version of the local option, then they will break you. At worst, from their point of view, you will be left as a divided and reactionary lump that carries on for another ten years or so but that knows in its heart of hearts that it has been defeated. At best, you will get up and leave. If that occurs they will be delighted. They will close the doggy-door behind you as soon as your tail disappears. You are betting the store at this point on the fact that they will be generous and let you go with your property. Rest assured they will not want to give you that option. At that point they will be no-holes-barred committed to canon law. A couple of smart lawyers will stop you in your tracks in having access to the assets of The United Methodist Church. Have you considered that as an alternative scenario?

EVANGELICAL   It has certainly cropped up in informal conversation. I can imagine the back-room gossip that would show up in some progressive circles around this topic.

TRADITIONALIST   It will do you the world of good to dwell on that imaginary back-room gossip. Let me get back, however, to my main line of thinking. I know folk hate the language of warfare but I am astonished at another element in your initial stance. You are starting out on the assumption that you have already lost. I have lost count of the number of wonderful United Methodist pastors who say we have lost the battle in the culture at large and need to make peace with it by accommodating in our church to the new reality. They are done with the dog-fight. Both you and these fine pastors (many see themselves as reluctant centrists) are going in with the white flag of surrender before you even begin. You have forgotten that the progressives and their allies have lost the debate and the vote in the church after forty years of full-court pressure. They have lost again and again and again. They now know that they cannot win the vote. If anything is certain, the majorities against them are going to increase. In these circumstances they want us all to believe that they can win this time around. They want us to forget what really happened and give in to our worst fears and anxieties about the future. They need to be upbeat in order to rally the troops and keep folk engaged.

EVANGELICAL   True, indeed. But look at the court cases of the last few years and the continued agitation and bullying across the committees of the church! They have found ways to exercise the local option without winning the vote. They have puts boots on the ground and are simply winning by fiat rather than by the normal procedures of our church.

TRADITIONALIST   There is a lot of premature celebration and not a little wishful thinking in progressive circles. Every time they lose they make these prophecies about the positive prospects next time around. However, like the Tea Party in our secular politics they tend to overestimate their strength and may yet make a serious blunder by over-reaching. I am not underestimating the significance of the new coalition that is in the making but the game is not at all over. We are heading for the United Methodist Superbowl in 2016 and we are now getting into the Playoffs.

EVANGELICAL   You really are mean to try the analogy with the Tea Party. Most of these folk are Yellow-dog Democrats.

TRADITIONALIST   Be that as it may. The point to registrar is that you are standing for the teaching and practices of The United Methodist Church. To be sure they offer their wooly verbiage and slogans as to how they are the true bearers of United Methodist identity. In an instant they know how to knock you off your balance. Many look upon orthodoxy as heresy and heresy as orthodoxy. They accuse you of being slave to a vile ideology all the while they themselves are ideological to the core. Notice how they get royally offended when someone challenges them. They are not interested in our constitutional standards of doctrine; they have either picked up or invented their own wobbly version of United Methodism. They cherry-pick their quotations from

John Wesley about the catholic spirit but conveniently ignore the small print. Or they tell us how many generations of Methodist preachers have been in their family, as if Methodism came with some kind of genetic code you got from your grandmother. Have you not noticed that underneath the surface many of them are often alienated from the church they claim to love and serve; some are really at breaking point. Some would bolt in a minute if one of their bishops led the charge in their conference to leave or a couple of the flagship local churches they control bailed out and set out on their own. They know in their bones that The United Methodist Church is a connectional body. You stand for the Connection; they do not. So stand your ground as the first step forward.

EVANGELICAL   But many of our folk feel as alienated as they do. They too are at breaking point.

TRADITIONALIST   Yes, of course. But hear me out. Your political opponents are no longer United Methodists. The will deny this on nine Bibles, repeatedly and in unison. However, here is the truth of the matter. They refuse to order their lives by our doctrine and discipline. At the end of day, that is something you need to remember. They disrupt our meetings and conferences. They separate themselves from us with their liturgical dress code. They turn every occasion into an opportunity to further their cause. They find their way into positions of power and influence and blackball those who disagree with them whenever they can. Think of what they will do at our meeting in the Rainbow Republic of Portland. Some of those involved in the struggle are within an inch of being fascists. They can even become fanatics who are prepared to burn themselves in public for the cause. These are not the people of reason and high moral standing they profess to be. They have absolutely no intention of backing down. Most of them are incapable of emptying their minds to make room for a single alien thought. Can you name one leader who has changed his or her mind? Have you ever seen them make any concession in dialogue sessions? I doubt it. Now of course, there are distinctions between moderates and radicals; the more sophisticated leaders know that they have their own crazy elements.

There are many wonderfully sincere and honest folk who are a delight to know; but you need to be clear that the personal is not the political. There is a complex coalition that they manage with remarkable skill. I give them this: they are Cadillac politicians. However, here is the question you have to face. Do you really want to hand your church over to this narrow-minded faction in United Methodism? Are you prepared to give away the store to those who have used every strategy at their disposal to impose their will on The United Methodist Church? I am certainly not going to do this. Indeed, I am not going to take even a first step in this direction.

EVANGELICAL   Keep going. I am listening.

TRADITIONALIST   Forgive me if I get a bit carried away. If truth be told, the progressives as a whole are a Trojan horse whose hidden inner army will destroy the church we love. They offer their horse as a great gift but do not be deceived; it has lethal weaponry on board. Their views on sexuality are the norming norm of everything that comes up for discussion. Follow some of their posts on Facebook and you will see what I mean. They are obsessed with their political agenda. They present us all with a chalice that will poison the whole life of the church from top to bottom. They have delivered a bomb that comes wrapped up in parcel with a postmark from peace with justice but rest assured it will blow the whole buildings apart in due course.

EVANGELICAL   I do sometimes worry that these folk are not in the least interested in salvation as either scripture or Wesley understand it. Everything gets reduced to their political agenda and whatever it takes to support it theologically and morally. To be sure, they sincerely repeat the slogans of the last generation about grace, but it is all so thin it is hard to see how this could ever convert anyone. They speak the language of Wesley and Method-ism but they mispronounce it. They read the same scripture as we do but where we see a glorious Savior and Lord they see a prophet who conveniently echoes their own agenda. Where we see a glorious King they see a rag doll painted with their bright red lipstick. However, it is clear that these folk really annoy you at a deep level. Isn't this a dangerous mood to entertain if you want

45

to take the measure of what is going on?

TRADITIONALIST   Of course it is. There is always the risk of misrepresenting your opponent's true position when you reach for strong language to describe what is really taking place. It is not easy to awaken folk who want to avoid conflict at any cost to come to grips with reality. There is also the risk of over-reacting. No doubt this is one reason why bishops and other leaders work overtime to keep the public conversation as short and as nice as possible. They immediately get uncomfortable if anybody begins to apportion blame for what has happened in our church over the last forty years. They blow secret fuses if there is even a hint of strong, straight-forward language in public or in print. They are scared stiff that this or that group might take offense. They mean well but everybody knows intuitively which group in the room is going to take offense; and these groups never fail to rise to the occasion. So the farrago of false pretenses never stops. As a result we engage in sham conversations most of the time. The more dangerous result is that we cannot face up to what is really happening and then sort through what to do. We never get below the surface and come to grips with what is really going on and so the problem simply gets worse. There is no possibility of repentance if we never face up to the reality of sin in our midst. You can never heal the body if you ignore the gaping wounds.

EVANGELICAL   Yet in private we all tell it like it is.

TRADITIONALIST   This reminds me of an issue that could take all day. So given my current mood, let me be blunt with you. Have you begun to think through how any plan to separate will impact our ethnic minorities? In Texas we have a new conference being formed, the Rio Texas Conference. So let's just focus on the Hispanic members of our church. They have just joined a majority white conference and now they will be faced all over again with what to do if the church does split. The perception on their part is that the evangelical groups are at best look-warm as far as their interests are concerned. They generally stand with you on doctrine and on gay marriage but they cannot stand with you on your conservative economic agenda and on immigration. Will they not inadvertently be confronted with the option of assimilation to your conservative political agenda or of going off again into the wilderness and starting all over again in a new denomination? Have you thought about the unbelievable upheaval they will face?

EVANGELICAL   We are beginning to tackle this. We are absolutely clear in our overall intention. We would want a church that would be a big tent that will absolutely include our ethnic brothers and sisters. We also recognize that there are landmines at every turn in the road. At the moment we are a voluntary group and we honestly do not know how the leadership and rank and file will stack up in terms of ethnic and even class diversity. Every group will have a different set of factors to weigh as we go through the planning process and on to the final decision. For those who are thoroughly Wesleyan in the Hispanic world the decision in part will boil to this. How far do the racial tensions and the economic factors they rightly perceive as important outweigh the challenge posed by the end of United Methodism? I think that the stakes are that high and it would be foolhardy to predict how things might turn out. This will clearly require systematic attention as we go forward.

TRADITIONALIST   Here is something else to ponder. If you do not take the kind of stand I am proposing what are you actually saying to those outside the United States who have saved the day from the beginning? Where is the gratitude we owe them? Are we going to leave them in the lurch? If the progressives and compatibilists succeed then the consequences for most of Africa, Eastern Europe, and Russia will be disastrous. We cannot even contemplate such a possibility. Rest assured the progressive lobby will be doing all they can to confuse and discredit these faithful United Methodists. I heard one bishop say recently that these people need to grow up. When the debate was still alive in the Episcopal Church Bishop Spong said at one of the Lambeth meetings that these people were still living in the Dark Ages. This is a global campaign and they will send subtle messages about money that will give many folk from outside the United States cause to pause and maybe go neutral. We cannot walk away from our brothers and sisters.

EVANGELICAL   We are already building that assumption into our plans for the future. There is no way we will walk away from our brothers and sisters who have saved the day across the last generation. It makes me really angry to see some progressives talk a good talk about the terrible effects of colonialism and then turn around and treat these members as if they were their house maids and yardmen. They are hypocrites on steroids in the way they act. We get all this sweet talk about inclusion until somebody shows up who does not share their agenda.

TRADITIONALIST   Splendid. It is about time that you woke up and got angry about what is happening. Jesus got angry when he saw wrong being done in the temple of his day. Paul was not your nice, wooly United Methodist who wants to sit in the middle and call for peace and reconciliation. If he had been all palsy-walsy and nice to those Celts in Galatia it would have been a disaster. These calls for peace when there is no peace are mechanisms of control and intimidation. They are like contraceptive pills that cut off our speech and thought at conception. Stop taking the pill! Angry operates as a moral detector for us at times. We have been bred out of the stronger moral emotions and turned into full-dress exhibitions of niceness and geniality. So here is the first part of my solution. We already have in our *Book of Discipline* provisions where an Annual Conference can leave and where a local church can leave The United Methodist Church. Rather than develop some grand plan of separation let's look at these regulations and provide an exit ramp for the disruptive dissidents in our midst. I have no mind for letting them go with their property; they certainly have no right to it; if they get their way rest assured they will want to hold on to the last piece of toilet paper. I would love to be proven wrong on this point. Maybe you could convince me to amend our current canon law to let them go with their property but frankly I am in no mood to do so. Make sure they pay their apportionments to the last day and then let them go and build their own progressive denomination with their own money.

EVANGELICAL   I am glad that you remain open to finding a way for them to go with their property. There may still be the remnants of a gracious, conciliatory Methodist heart beating in your breast. There is only one problem: these folk are not going to leave; they have said so again and again. Given their systematic disregard of our canon law to date, there isn't a snowball's chance in hell of their being bound by such legislation. Even on your own understanding the revised legislation would leave its deployment entirely voluntary; and we know they will refuse to exercise that option. They know all too well that they would be another mainline minority report in the culture of the West and they would rather walk over broken glass in bare feet to General Conference that let this happen! They will sit tight and the war will go on.

TRADITIONAL   My second part addresses this worry. We need to shore up our regulations. The deployment of the just resolution is an utter sham. We need to take it to the Judicial Council and have it overturned. From the beginning we have been a church that heeded Paul's admonition to do all things decently and in order. Heavens above, we ordain clergy to take responsibility for good order in the church. This game is not over yet. We also need to introduce legislation to tackle the problem of dissident bishops. As individuals these are wonderful people. I know some of them personally and on a one-to-one they are the real deal. However, these very same people can readily be a menace to the life of the church when they buy into the progressive agenda. It is just as bad when they sit on their hands and try to muddle through. This whole idea of biblical obedience is a joke. They have turned language on its head, claiming to use disobedience as a form of obedience. If some of your folk protested by getting their local church to withhold their apportionments, they would soon feel the reach of their bishop's wrath. They would not hear a word about biblical obedience. It would be cries of disobedience all the way to the Backofbeyond. You know that they use appointments as a form of punishment; they have been doing this for years. Not all the time of course, but when they want to bring a wayward pastor into line, that is clearly one of their options. How's that for a version of the local option! They will pack you off to Ballygobackwards in a heartbeat. That's what the local option means for them. I know you can give chapter and verse here.

EVANGELICAL   You bet I could.

TRADITIONALIST   Bishops in their office as bishop must be held accountable. We have a host of good legal minds that can come up with a solution. In fact our Constitution clearly states that the General Conference has the direct authority to provide for their discontinuance because of inefficiency or unacceptability. All we may need to do is to find a mechanism that will allow this to happen expeditiously. We should also look at abolishing Jurisdictions over time, but that will need more long-term thinking. We must be careful not to overload the legislative agenda. For now we should go through the *Book of Discipline* inch by inch and fix it where it needs fixing. Once the progressives realize we mean business they will come under increasing pressure to leave. As I mentioned earlier, it would not take much for the dike to open up and the waters to flow. They think they have found the wedge that can crack the whole thing wide open; They may have actually invented the sword on which they may fall. Even if we fail in the end, somebody needs to stand up and make sure they have to battle for every inch of territory they take over. This is not a matter of teaching some self-righteous leaders a lesson. It is simply a matter of good house-keeping.

EVANGELICAL   So you are asking us to go back into trench warfare one more time? I am not sure we are up for this. It is exhausting and extremely expensive business. We do have folk who love this kind of thing; they seem to know the *Book of Discipline* better than they know the Bible. All that said, I am delighted if you and others take up this agenda and succeed.

TRADITIONAL   It is indeed exhausting! And I have a third element in my solution. Consider a parallel case. In the nineteenth century English Methodism faced a doctrinal crisis of enormous proportions when Adam Clarke, that remarkable Irishman from Portstewart, went off the rails theologically. In the name of biblical authority and reason he denied the eternal generation of the Son from the Father. He railed against the doctrine of the Trinity and was totally incorrigible. Clarke was one of our very best as scholar, evangelist, missionary, and fundraiser. However, the English Methodist Church kept its nerve; they acted prudently and took the long view. As Methodists generally never do, they did not excommunicate him. However, they did not let his sons or disciples enter the ministry; and they set about articulating a positive account and defense of their commitment to the Trinity.

EVANGELICAL   Good heavens! I thought Adam Clarke was one of ours. I have his multi-volume commentary of scripture in my library.

TRADITIONALIST   Good for you; at times he can be brilliant; at other times he is a tight-fisted rationalist. However, take note of what I am proposing. We need to go back to work theologically. We need a robust theology of ecclesial suffering. There is a very heavy cross to be borne here. You yourself can quote those amazing texts from Paul that speak to this. We need a constructive vision of sexual morality that deals with the fragility of our lives in this arena and with an attractive account of marriage. And, yes, we need to think through why we permit divorce and do not see it as on the level of homosexual practice; the pastoral theology of Eastern Orthodox has much to teach us on this score. Sin abounds, but so too does grace and redemption. Above all, we need a theology of our identity as a church that will refresh our mission and ministry. We can start with our constitutional standards and revisit the golden era of Methodist theology in the nineteenth century. My own hunch is that we need a robust doctrine of the church that follows the order in the creed and rests on an industrial-strength account of the work of the Holy Spirit. There is risk in this, to be sure, for it is easy to make the Holy Spirit an empty cypher that can be filled with all sorts of silly nonsense. As a bonus this latter kind of work will get us beyond the utter failure of ecumenism over the last century. Think of all that excitement after Vatican II. It has all gone up in smoke with division stalking the land once again.

EVANGELICAL   Whatever we do, I can sign on to the last assignment. We have some good scholars who could help on this score. If we divide we will have our work cut out for us forming a new church. I am not sure I have gotten the full picture but at least you are now putting flesh on a plan of action. And I appreciate your candor now that our other friends have gone off to organize for the next General Conference. I do have one last question. If this option does not work, will you come with us?

TRADITIONALIST   Go ahead and work up your plans. I am not for separation but life is full of terrible surprises so despite my harsh language I will not frown on having all the options on the table. Perhaps we do need the nuclear option after all. Let's exchange emails and we can talk about this when the time is ripe.

Dialogue IV

A Wobbly Start in Planning for the Immediate Future

PROGRESSIVE   It is such a relief to have had Evangelical and Traditional leave us. I have to confess, however, that it is embarrassing to be in the same room as Pietist. Maybe I should put on my rainbow stole and put up a selfie on Facebook so that my friends will not misunderstand and think that I am compromising my position. I am more comfortable with Reconciler, but even then we have to look at the small print. Let me be clear at the outset. There is no going back to some kind of creedal orthodoxy on my part. Nor are we going to back down on full inclusion in our church. The policy of don't ask, don't tell with respect to doctrine is great and has served us well once you make it through the Boards of Ordained Ministry; but that strategy is dead on arrival on the gay issues.

PIETIST   I am not sure any longer who my friends really are. There is not much I can do now that I am out in the open with my change of mind on gay marriage; all I can do is keep our feet to the fire on being charitable to one another. It was a very heavy cross to bear listening to the hectoring of Traditional and his dualistic ways of thinking. Evangelical was not far behind. Yet I detect a real change of attitude there. Maybe there is hope for some of them. As I mentioned earlier, I could follow the party line with the best of them. To be honest, I even enjoyed the fight. But thank God that I am no longer like one of those conservatives who are so judgmental and legalistic. Those days are over. Maybe I should develop a prayer in the style of the great Cranmer that would capture my deliverance from that way of thinking.

RECONCILER   I appreciate your pain but we have work to do. It is going to be a hard sell at General Conference to get my proposal through. Let's think through together where we can go from here.

First Steps in Self-Identification

PIETIST   Before we go there would you mind if we took a moment and I got some help from Progressive. I do not want to hog the conversation or be uncharitable in any way, but I do have some questions about homosexual practices that puzzle me. Please understand that all I want to be is loving and caring and truly spiritual. You know I have been reading all this wonderful material from the patristic period and from the Desert Fathers and Mothers. I am something of an expert now on spirituality myself, or at least that's what my friends keep telling me. I am trying to be humble about this sort of talk. It would be a bit odd for me to speak of my humility, of course. I am working on that too after my revelation from the Spirit. You know this is not easy for someone who came from background; those old self-righteous, judgmental videos keep running in my head. Looking back I can see that I was in a state of bondage myself. It was terrible. I am so glad that I am no longer like the dreadful conservative I once was. Maybe I should look into the whole topic of demon harassment. Maybe we should think about providing spiritual therapy free of charge to the conservatives. Traditional may need a full-scale exorcism. The Vatican runs a seminar on this now for two weeks. Wouldn't it be wonderful to take advantage of two weeks in Rome and get deeper into spirituality by visiting the great churches and the catacombs? Our real problem is lack of piety and spirituality. This was the genius of Wesley and early Methodism. We really need to get back to prayer and fasting and the study of real piety and spirituality. And don't forget the round, mahogany tables and seeking the discernment of the Spirit and coming together in love and care for one another.

PROGRESSIVE   I am afraid the hair is rising on the back of my neck as you go on and on about your version of spirituality. Maybe this whole effort to get together is hopeless. I am all into spirituality, but I cringe when I hear you speak in the way you do. It turns out to be so artificial and superficial and inward-looking and individualistic. I haven't a clue how to use all that language about regeneration, justification, entire sanctification, the witness of the spirit, latitudinarianism, and the whole bagful of the language of Zion that Wesley used in the eighteenth century. It gives me a headache just to spell the words. What we need is a transformative spirituality that tackles the real problem we face. That was what Wesley was all about. The real issue here is harmful speech, discrimination, and oppression. I much prefer a spirituality that works with fresh, creative images, liturgical dance, and dialogical sermons. It was a real coup for us when we managed to get that kind of worship and spirituality at the last General Conference. I loved the way the worship expert we managed to slip into the arrangements developed the theme of the ocean, and water, and space. Most folk never knew that she was fully on board with our agenda. I love the way the Virginia Annual Conference has introduced us to the liturgy of the Native Americans when we meet on their lands. I was so touched in my heart when I heard the drums and the invocation of the spirits asking for permission for us to meet. It was so much more liberating that invoking the patriarchal God of orthodoxy with all that oppressive language of Father and Son. We need a whole new language to capture the experience of the spirit as we know it today. That means we need a spirituality of everyday experience. I read a wonderful book on the plane on the journey over here that insists that God is really most present to us in our doubts and darkness and in the suffering of the oppressed. We need to capture that in our worship and spirituality.

PIETIST   You must give me the name of that book before I leave. I have to say that I love the old classical, orthodox liturgies. They enrich my own personal devotions. I noticed that some of your progressives love them too. I suspect that many of them do not believe the content the way I do; in fact it puzzles me that they are so conservative and High-Church liturgically.

PROGRESSIVE   It only puzzles you because you take it all so literally like fundamentalists would if they used them. We take it figuratively. We sing it rather than say it. Surely you can understand that some of our folk still love the beautiful language of the past. I love it too on the big occasions of the Christian year. Using the old liturgies is also a salutary way of keeping our congregations from knowing too early on where we stand on the issues we are fighting for. We come across as so traditional and orthodox on everything else that few really notice how radical we are. Some of us belong to that older generation of liberals who paved the way for my generation and created space for us in the church. But to come back to my point, I don't deny that we meet the divine in lovely sunsets and beautiful music and in moments of sexual intimacy. All that is true, especially the presence of God in sexual intimacy, which is one reason I cannot understand why anyone would want to stop our homosexual brothers and sisters having sex. They meet God there just as much as straight people do. Our old liberal teachers made much of the slogan that if God is not present everywhere God is not present anywhere, and they loved to preach about sunsets and great music as revelations of the divine. Yet they had a hard time adjusting to our language about God and they were real prudes when it came to sex. It was so much fun to see them sweat, and squirm, and blush when we talked openly about sex. They thought we were being vulgar when we adopted the salty language that went along with our liberation from the white middle-brow taboos. Thank God for the sexual revolution of the sixties! And thank God for the liberation theologians who came after them and challenged the old neo-liberal dinosaurs and then taught us that we find God first and foremost among the marginalized, the poor, and the oppressed.

RECONCILER   I have to confess that I am not fully on board with these new ways of thinking. At the end of the day I suppose I am really what used to be called a liberal evangelical before the fundamentalists stole the term and made it their own. Back in the nineteen thirties I am told that there were even a group who self-identified as liberal evangelicals in Scotland and England. It included folk like James S. Stewart and Bishop Stephen Neil. That is why the term 'conservative evangelical' got picked up; the fundamentalists then simply dropped the relevant adjectives and high-jacked the term 'evangelical'. I don't think that you are entirely fair to the great liberal Protestants of the twentieth century. I started out in another world, the world of the fundamentalism and Pentecostalism, and I needed to learn how to think for myself. The liberals were wonderful people who insisted on clarity, proper academic method, historical criticism, respect for other religions, serious philosophy, good judgments in ethics, and intellectual courage in facing the challenges of modernity. I cannot tell you how liberating it was to go to a school where this was the norm. I loved it. They got it right on the race issue. They marched with Martin Luther King Jr.. One of them wrote a book dealing with the criticisms he got from the first wave of liberation theology. Most if not all of them are progressive on the gay issue as well. This is one reason any idea of schism is totally anathema to me. Imagine a church where we lose the folk who are committed to scholarship and criticism. It would be a disaster. We have to learn to agree to disagree. That was essential to the legacy they left us. We need everybody holding together if we are to arrive at the truth in the academy and in the church. I love that slogan about open doors, open hearts, open minds that the advertising people developed. That was worth every cent we spent on it. It gets us away from the language of censure and denunciation and sends a clear message that all are welcome. I saw a big church in Texas recently that had that message in its welcome booth in the parking lot. I immediately sent a text to our communications expert to make sure that we did that too. We have a big sign out on the highway now proclaiming that all are welcome. We really mean all.

PROGRESSIVE   You really do need a further update. I hope you can get beyond the thinking of those white patriarchal males. I agree that they created room for my own teachers, but some of those liberals are still living and are having second thoughts about what they did. They thought that they were giving us a seat at the table. Little did they realize that we had every intention of taking over the table!   When the truth dawned on them, they took off into retirement and into the sunset. Some of them really cannot stand us despite our agreements on the gay issue. They have no clue about what is involved in transformative, liberating scholarship and teaching. Deep down they were white European males loaded up with self-delusions about objectivity and neutrality that oppressed women for centuries. They could never get beyond that. We believe in organic scholarship where the goal is not to understand the world but to change it.

RECONCILER   I understand. Give me a list of books that could help me come to terms with these new ideas. They were just coming on the scene the year before I graduated. It will help me understand some of these younger clergy who are on my staff and that I am trying to mentor. I will need to get up to speed on this if we are to succeed in the new seminary I am working with after the collapse of the one next door. I am very excited about what we can do there in transforming United Methodism and making it fit for purpose in the twenty-first century.

PROGRESSIVE   I will be glad to help. However, that was not the main point I wanted to make, important though it may be. Your remarks about our popular slogan was beginning to make my blood boil and I needed to step back a moment before delivering my soul. Think of the sheer hypocrisy of that slogan. We have been slamming the door shut in the faces of our gay brothers and sisters for over a generation and we dare to send this message to the general public! We have had enough of this accommodation to bigotry, prejudice, ignorance, and ways of thinking that belong to the Dark Ages.

RECONCILER   All I wanted to do was say a good word on behalf of our liberal teachers. As you know by now I really mean it when I say that we are open to all. I am on your side on the gay issue. So can we get back to the reason why we met and start working on what we might do?

PIETIST   I am so sorry I led us astray. I just wanted to get some help from Progressive on some of the things I have heard about homosexual practice. I suspect that I may be a bit naïve but I am willing to learn. As you know, I have been through a season of illumination and repentance and all I want to be is to be charitable, loving, and caring. Do forgive me again for leading us astray. I am so sorry. I will ask God to help me not do that again. It goes against everything I believe about the grace of God and the need for charitable discourse and the round table.

Progressives in Action

PROGRESSIVE   I am not sure I want to give away all the secrets of the operations we are planning but let me see if I can list some of them. This will get the ball rolling. Then we can hear what you might have in mind. We divide our strategy into three levels. First, we want to change the culture of our church much as we and our allies did in the wider culture. You can read up on how they did it in law, psychiatry, natural science, psychology, education, the military, the business world, Hollywood, and the media. We nearly knocked that stupid reality TV show by those dreadful duck people from Louisiana off the television networks. We are still working on the Boy Scouts; but the die is cast and we will soon take care of that group as well. We crossed another line when we managed to get our President to raise the issue of gay rights with the Russians at the Winter Olympics. We have now succeeded in getting our agenda embedded in our foreign policy. What all this does is give us some super-powerful tailwinds when we come to changing our church. Time and history are on our side. The arc of destiny is bending in our direction. This gives us great hope for the future whatever the initial setbacks. Even the evangelicals are beginning to break ranks. I gather that George Soros and various foundations have been helping educate them by offering money if they join the network of interest groups that are out there beating the drum for open societies and for justice across the world. I really do not know that the full story but maybe you folk represent that growing edge yourself.

RECONCILER   Let me assure you that I have come to my position entirely on my own through careful study and reflection. I never got a penny from anyone. And I am hoping that the budget in my local church for the future will hold as it stands. Winning this vote will take care of this because I can then claim the full official backing of The United Methodist Church. We would then have the whole of mainline Protestantism behind us. You could never put a price-tag on the credibility that such backing gives us.

PROGRESSIVE   Isn't it a shame that we have such narrow-minded believers in United Methodism!   These are power-hungry bigots who use the threat of withholding finances in order to keep control. If we did not have to deal with them we would have moved years ago in the early nineties and struck all the hurtful language from our discipline. Some people really are slow learners. Even then, our opponents failed to see that our very identity as mainline Protestant is a godsend. There is a very useful narrative in play here. 'Mainline' means that you are on the journey represented by the Episcopalians, the Lutherans, the Presbyterians, the United Church of Christ, the National Council of Churches, and the like. We are on the same road that they are on with a clear beginning, middle, and end. Our goal is to have one more shove to get us across the finishing line. Despite all the setbacks we are sure we can get there in 2016 at the next General Conference. We are right now stuck in the middle and it is a terrible burden to bear when we talk to our colleagues in the other churches.

RECONCILER   I think of myself in the middle, not the muddled middle, of course, but the strategic middle. I belong to that middle group that knows how to rise above the two extremist groups who constantly want to hog the limelight. It is time that the great middle ground in United Methodism stood up and took over our church and fixed it once and for all. I really mean business this time around. I am not going home from General Conference again with my tail between my legs.

PROGRESSIVE   I hope you are not counting me among the extremists!   We are just standing up for civil rights, non-discrimination, and the end of oppression. You have to make a real choice here and get out of the middle and stand on the side of history.

RECONCILER   I think we may be talking past one another here. You were referring to the middle of a journey. I am talking about the crucial political grouping that needs to stand up and be counted and help me take The United Methodist Church to a better future. We agree that the tailwinds are behind us all across the culture so let's get back to the review of your plans.

PROGRESSIVE   Let me see where I was. Yes, I was talking about the first level of influence. We want to change the culture of United Methodism. The second level is doing all we can to discredit the opposition. This means talking frankly in our own circles about them and who they really are. They are bigoted, ignorant, superstitious, backward, power-hungry, resentful, hateful, legalistic, homophobic, orthodox, and generally nasty. You will find if one of these adjectives does not fit another will. If they offer an olive branch, take it, play along, and then use it against them. All this we keep to ourselves. The crucial strategy in the public arena is to frame the debates in such a way that they will be seen as the dividers and not the reconcilers. This is the public impression we want to get across to as many people as possible, in as many ways as possible, as often as possible. Hammer away at it in season and out of season. On this I think we have already won the war. The bishops never speak up on their behalf; they are scared stiff of being associated with folk who are already tarred and feathered as splitters and dividers. If a bishop steps out of line their own staff will reprimand them. Everything the opposition says and does is received with a hermeneutic of suspicion. Sometimes they are so stupid that they play right into our narrative about them.

RECONCILER   I fully understand the communicative arts behind what you are saying but to be honest this whole approach leaves a bad taste in my mouth. But carry on.

PROGRESSIVE   Another ploy in discrediting them is to paint them as opposed to reason, experience, and science. Unfortunately, they have made real progress in undermining the Quadrilateral but it is still on the books and some of them love it. It gives them a way to distance themselves from fundamentalism. One crucial element in our strategy is to insist on testimonies from our gay brothers and sisters. It is very hard to argue against experience when it is presented with flair. Our opponents get fidgety and uncomfortable; it sort of knocks them off the intellectual case they want to make. When you have testimonies that speak of the terrible suffering that gay people have to face, you take the strategy to a whole new level. Show a graphic PowerPoint of the statistics about teenage suicides, work in stories about harassment, and then drive it home by making it clear that they are complicit in all this suffering and violence. By the way, when you have Annual Conference events around the gay debate, make sure that if it involves breakout sessions that you get listed first on the program and that you get the best hall available.

RECONCILER   I am doing the best I can to stay up with you here.

PROGRESSIVE   The third level of strategy is more narrowly political. I can be brief here. There are three basic points to make. First, get as many from the progressive side as possible elected at the Annual Conferences as delegates to General Conference. Spare no effort to get the women clergy to do their part. Figure out how to make the right lists and to get the texting system down between votes. Try to get as near the top of the delegation as possible. That helps in the election of progressive bishops as well, of course. Make sure that you take into account full inclusion; so network with the various ethnic groups to ensure that the right people get elected. Keep out those female clergy who are on the wrong side and do the same to exclude individuals in the ethnic minority who might be suspect. Happily, we have already ostracized the female conservative clergy; they just stay away from the women clergy groups or form their own little reactionary cabals. Happily, too we can rely for the most part on ethnic minorities. They know what it is like to suffer discrimination. They rightly associate our cause with the extension of the civil rights movement. Maybe that belongs at the first level but it fits here too. Now here is the second point. Alongside the elections, work on getting the right resolutions passed in as many Annual Conferences as possible. We have a terrific data base of people that we can network. And the third strategy is obvious. Once we get to General Conference we make sure that we have our people placed in the right legislative committees to get our resolutions to the floor of General Conference in the second week. The details need not detain us at this stage; we have folk who just love working out how to get this done.

Undermining Church Law and Disruptive Demonstrations

RECONCILER   I notice that you have not mentioned the more radical sides of your strategy. What about the move to undermine church law? And what about using disruptive demonstrations? These are tactics that are generally associated with the progressive wing of the church, aren't they.

PROGRESSIVE   I like the use of the term 'associated' here. I really wanted to paint the big picture here and this does not involved disruptive demonstrations. We do not stand up and condemn them, of course. That would be unwise given the effective role they can play. What happens is this. We have groups within our groups who organize their own sub-plots and strategies. Many of these are more local. It is a bit like having a franchise with local owners. They operate with our brand but we do no own or control the operations. In fact we would not even try to control what goes on for you never know what can develop when emotions run high and people begin to hold demonstrations. Remember the time that fellow from West Texas seized the communion vessels and smashed them in public. That really hurt our cause. What we do is co-ordinate with the bishops and other officers of the church to broker deals as best we can. So we actually provide a brake on some of the more radical members of our coalition. So I am not proposing that we take up that element in the overall strategy that gets developed.

RECONCILER   I am so relieved. Perhaps that is why some on my side want to label you as an extremist on a par with the Tea Party crowd among the conservative extremists. There is no way I will be party to that kind of action. No way whatsoever! It runs counter to my role as a reconciler between the groups that are tearing us apart. I suspect that your moves to undermine church law may fall in the same ballpark.

PROGRESSIVE   Maybe so. But let me explain. Our strategy to undermine church law on the ground is not one we are prepared to give up. Look at it this way. We have been working for over a generation to change the vote and we have gotten nowhere. So we do what any interest group does when it is confronted with unjust law. We challenge the law by ignoring it, trimming its sails, pitting it against other elements we can find in the law, providing legal aid in the courts of the church, and making sure that any punishment is purely trivial. Of course, this is not something we can control. Folk like our courageous Bishop Talbert acted on his own for conscience's sake. I am thrilled at the heroism of those clergy who in what may be the last days of their lives run the risk of being defrocked. Given their age and their health it takes a really hard heart to put them on trial. For the most part we simply talk over these cases, consider other ways of undermining unjust laws, and then let events take their course. We do not want to control these kinds of things; we support them when they happen and we let them evolve. So you might say that we welcome them but do not want to control them.

RECONCILER   Forgive me if I press you here. Are you in favor of breaking church law as it currently stands?

PROGRESSIVE   Yes. I think I have said as much. Yes, definitely, yes.

RECONCILER   And if you were in position, say, as a bishop, would you break or nullify or mitigate church law if you found yourself in an opportune situation where you could do so?

PROGRESSIVE   Yes, I would. But now you are putting events within my control. As I say, our level of control on this front more generally is extremely limited. We leave that to individuals and sub-groups, and we will provide such support as may be helpful. Let me repeat an earlier point. We are absolutely in favor of breaking church law as a strategy of last resort. We now live at a time where a strategy of last resort is upon us. We have tried every which way to change church law and been defeated every time. So there it stands with us. I suppose if you want a straight answer it is right to say that we stand in theory and in practice for breaking church law at this time in the struggle.

RECONCILER   Fair enough. I understand where you are coming from. For me, this is not an option. There are too many people in the middle I would lose if I went down this road. It would be seen as a total accommodation to the progressive wing of the church. As I keep saying again and again to my critics, this is not where we are. We want to uphold church law until it is changed. This is an uncomfortable place to occupy. The way forward is to change the law of the church and then uphold it. I am convinced we can achieve this in a way that will bring an end to our fighting. We develop the local option as outlined in our open letter to the church. I can tell you at this point that we have hundreds of people who are signing on online. Believe me, this is the issue that will be on the table at General Conference. We will make this happen; and we will win this time around.

PROGRESSIVE   Tell me more about how you intend to achieve this? My friends tell me that I seem to look on politics as an exciting blood sport. I do not like the imagery but there days when this description haunts me.

Reconciliation in Action

RECONCILER   You speak in the future tense, as you should, but there is also a personal backstory. As you may know, I am fearless about taking on controversial issues that speak to people where they are. I have worked out a system whereby my sermons become popular books that sell like hot cakes with the DVD's that go along with them. The crucial barrier to changing the law of our church on homosexuality is the Bible. I am learning that feminists discovered this point a generation ago and realized they had to tackle its place in the culture as a source of oppression and patriarchy. Now, I decided to kill two birds with one stone. So I did my normal thing by preaching and then publishing a book on the Bible. To the innocent reader this looked like my standard mode of operating. However, I took it one step further and made the Bible a factor on our side of the aisle rather than the conservative side of the aisle. I took away the primary weapon of the opposition. At the same time I was working away at writing up an initial proposal that would develop the local option. I then launched this in the virtual world and the immediate results are very encouraging.

65

PROGRESSIVE   I really wish we had folk on our side who could operate like this! But you make it sound like a one-man-band on a gigantic ego trip. Isn't this a very patriarchal, hierarchical way of thinking and operating? I am sure there must be critics of yours out there who love to point out that you are becoming more and more messianic as you get older. Another male messiah! Is this what is on offer?

RECONCILER   Believe me I have gotten wind of this sort of talk and it really hurts. I am no messiah. I am an enabler and a leader; a leader who works by enabling. I cover this kind of thing in my national seminars in my local church. Somebody has to step up and lead or we are headed over the cliff as we saw at last General Conference. This is just the way things are. Somebody has to lead, and organize, and get the votes together for the next General Conference. Call it whatever you like, but I am not backing off from fixing United Methodism. On this front I have lots of experience across the years. The first step was to get out ahead of the evangelical group that wants to split the church. I honestly think I took the wind out of their sails. At one level we all know who is behind their scheme to divide the church. At another level we do not know who they are. We have beaten them to the punch. They made a fatal mistake when they mentioned division in their press release. If you look carefully it is mentioned but not endorsed in the other document that was made public. From here on out they will be playing catch-up. And notice the number of evangelicals who have already come on board with us.

PROGRESSIVE   It sounds like a strategy of divide and conquer, to me. Not that I disagree with it for one moment, but we need to be honest here.

RECONCILER   Not at all. I lay out the local option and let the chips fall where they will. The next step is to develop the detailed legislative package and make sure it is as fool-proof as possible. This is by far the hardest part. You never know what a Judicial Council can do with what passes at General Conference. Which is one reason we need to cover that base too; we need our people on the Judicial Council to make sure it does not torpedoed at the last minute. We have to work through the system from top to bottom where it is. That part of the journey begins with detailed legislation. The pig picture is clear: let the material in current church law be the default position. Then let Annual Conferences decide if they want to opt out. Then let local churches decide if they want to opt out. All the rest can be worked out over the next calendar year by a small team that I will co-ordinate. Then it will be back to the church at large with a top-notch advertising campaign and a public relations exercise that will get the message across. But I am getting ahead of myself.

PROGRESSIVE   I am sure there are parts of the legislative work that we would want to help on. It might end up being our Plan B. We have some very savvy folk who are brilliant at drafting legislation for General Conference.

RECONCILER   The next step, or rather a parallel step, is to build a groundswell of support using social media. The days are gone when decisions are made by elected delegates. To be sure, they will be the ones who actually vote. But they do not work in a vacuum. They are human like the rest of us. If we can get our case out across the connection we can get a majority on board with us. Our delegates are good people who are looking for leadership and I am ready to take that on. Already other leaders are stepping forward to get things moving in the right direction. One big Texas Annual Conference has already elected their delegates because some folk there caught the vision and brought forward the date so that they could get ahead of the pack. The bloggers are now noting that this is going to be the most important General Conference since 1968. Those Texas leaders saw that they would need two years to get ready. They have a year to begin building the base for elections in other Annual Conferences and can already operate from a position of strength. This train has already left the station and there will be lots of points where others can get on.

PROGRESSIVE   I can already see that you have a plan that is very impressive. I am not sure I am still on board with the vision of leadership.

RECONCILER   Maybe a word of explanation will help. I

suppose I am what used to be called a big-steeple pastor. That language is now obsolete, of course, but there is a rough analogy. These folk have always been important in Methodism. They are the pool from which we draw many of our bishops and they have enormous influence on the way our church develops. Many of them have published as prolifically as I have if you look back across the last hundred years. So really, there is nothing new here.

PROGRESSIVE   That is one element that worries me. This is an old way of thinking and operating! This whole way of operating is so male-oriented and patriarchal. Where are the women and minorities?

RECONCILER   Check out the list of signature and you will see there are scores of them from some of our biggest churches. I hope you will go back and sign on too. If you look some of your people were really excited with my proposal and signed on immediately.

PROGRESSIVE   Now you are like all the other politicians and are trying to recruit me to your cause.

RECONCILER   A clever point on your part. And probably true to boot. However, there is one aspect of our situation that may help lessen the anguish. Where are our academics when we need them? Surely these should be stepping up to the plate and leading us in the effort to save United Methodism. I sometimes feel our academics have gone AWOL from the life of the church. Albert Outler was my hero from the first day I ever heard him speak. Traditionalist mentioned that Outler changed his mind on what he developed in the nineteen seventies but you have to admire his ability as a scholar and churchman. In a way there is a terrible vacuum of leadership in our church. Most of our academics, even if they are on the side of revision, really do not seem to care. Our council of bishops has been dysfunctional for a generation. So you surely understand why folk like me – and, mark me, I am not the only one – have to step into the vacuum and show some leadership.

PROGRESSIVE   We progressives prefer a much more collegial way of operating. This fits much more with the shift in the academic world that is now in place. In the old world the center of gravity revolved around those big white whales that flopped around the ocean in search of prey to a very different world where we work in terms of movements.

RECONCILER   I get it. However, I too see myself as part of a collaborative movement rather than out there as a lone-ranger trying to fix United Methodism all on my own. I like to think of myself as belonging to a third way, or to the extreme center, or to the strategic middle. I love banging around these new ideas about shifts in culture, but we really need to get back to figuring out where we go from here.

PIETIST   I am generally in agreement with Reconciler here. In fact I have just put a post on my website that draws attention to the initial documents he and others have launched. I really do not see myself as a politician but I will do all I can to make sure that our discourse is charitable and civil. However, I would like to go back to the issue I raised at the beginning about homosexual practice; somehow I cannot get it out of my head....

RECONCILER   I think we should stick to our agenda. I have several important phone calls to make to some of my colleagues across the country and I am worried that we will not get to the real work in hand. Can I try a summary statement of where we are?

PROGRESSIVE   Fire ahead. I am all ears.

A Summation

RECONCILER   We are agreed that we cannot go on as we are with the current language and legislation in the *Book of Discipline.*

PROGRESSIVE and PIETIST   Yes.

RECONCILER   We are agreed that there should be language that permits those who have been working for change to be able to move forward and exercise their conscience.

PROGRESSIVE AND PIETIST   Yes.

RECONCILER   We are not in agreement that this should be mandated for the whole church.

PROGRESSIVE   Agreed. I think it should be mandated for the whole church. I will not have a church where one part is undermining the injustice that the other part is seeking to secure. You clearly disagree with this.

RECONCILER   Now on the politics of the situation. We agree that we cannot continue as we are.

PROGRESSIVE AND PIETIST   Yes.

RECONCILER   We agree that we should organize to change the language in the *Book of Discipline.*

PROGRESSIVE AND PIETIST   Yes.

RECONCILER   We agree that we should engage in the conventional practices that have been used across the generations related to the election of delegates, drafting legislation, taking it up through committees to the floor of the General Conference, and forming coalitions high up and low down to get all this done.

PROGRESSIVE AND PIETIST   Yes.

RECONCILER   We do not agree on whether we should break current church law and on whether we should censure those who engage in disruptive demonstrations and political theatre.

PROGRESSIVE AND PIETIST   That is exactly right.

RECONCILER   Well that is as far as I think we can go for now. Indeed I think it is as far as we may need to go. Let's stay in touch as we move forward. Coalition building is now clearly an option for all of us and we can allow our respective teams to be in touch with each other.

PIETIST   Can I add a word? Surely we need to bathe this whole operation in prayer and fasting. We face extremely troubled waters up ahead and we will never get through this without the guidance and power of the Spirit. Would you mind if I gathered a group to make recommendations on this front that y'all can consider?

RECONCILER   Absolutely. Keep me in the loop.

PROGRESSIVE   I confess I have real reservations on this proposal. If we take up this option we really need to make sure that any joint effort will be inclusive and that we avoid oppressive, patriarchal language, and really come up with some truly creative liturgies. I hope you really caught how important this is to our folk. I propose we all wear our wonderful rainbow stoles. We should avoid harmful, divisive speech as we proceed. We need to send a very clear message in our liturgy that we are fully and irrevocably inclusive.

PIETIST   I will be glad to take this to the round table that I will bring together. This is certainly a fair and noble suggestion. Forgive me if I raise one other question. I am still bothered by the rumors I am hearing about homosexual practices. Can we take a minute to hear my concern before we leave?

RECONCILER   I hope you can keep this short. I really need to get on the phone and get in touch with my design team for moving forward.

A Fly in the Ointment

PIETIST   Let me see if I can get this out in the open. I know that for homosexual men, the conventional way to have sex is by having anal sex. It used to be called sodomy when I was growing up, but we no longer use that kind of uncharitable language nowadays. But I keep hearing that there are all sorts of other practices in which they engage and I would like to know more.

PROGRESSIVE   Now you have crossed a line. Let me give it to you straight. I started out being embarrassed in your presence. Now I am beyond embarrassment; I really am angry. I always felt your types were homophobes and now I see it for myself. You are a total and complete hypocrite. Have we ever asked you what you did in the privacy of your own bedroom with your wife? Come on! Cough up what you and your wife have gotten up to over the years when you had sex. Can you specify the various positions for us? What manuals did you hide from the children? Did you watch movies to get you in the mood? How many times a week

71

did you do it? Did you consult a sexual therapist? Let's start with this little list and see how far you will go! I am not sure I can stand to be in the same room as you! You creepy hypocrite!

RECONCILER   Hold on a minute. This is not going to help us make progress in getting a coalition together. We should stick to the political issues that brought us together in the first place.

PROGRESSIVE   Are you trying to shut me down and put certain subjects off limits? Our generation learned to be open and honest about sex. I am not afraid to deal with any topic that comes up. Is this going to be a dialogue or a monologue dominated by the alpha males of the tribe? Do we really have to listen to homophobic Pietist any longer?

PIETIST   Look, I was just trying to understand what I may be getting into when I began to sort through the divine revelation the Holy Spirit placed on my heart. I am new to this whole world and I really just wanted to raise the possibility of same sex marriage as an option we needed to look at.

PROGRESSIVE   So you are walking back all that talk about being in favor of gay marriage? Are you heading back into the badlands of Traditional and Evangelical? To use your pious phraseology, are you now repenting of your repentance? Are we getting a new revelation that cancels the earlier revelation?

PIETIST   Why do you have to be so aggressive? Why can't you be charitable and give me room to breathe? I am one of those folk who sometimes takes five steps forward and then two backwards and then one step forward and four steps backward.

PROGRESSIVE   So you really are changing your mind.

PIETIST   No. I am thinking this through out loud as best I can. I thought you would be someone who could and would help me. I began to search the internet but I ended up on sites that were not really fit for holy eyes. I asked my wife to help but she squirmed and mumbled something about being disgusted. At my age my hearing is beginning to go and I am not sure what she said. I could see she did not want to help. Maybe it is politically incorrect to raise this kind of question. If that is the case I am certainly willing to watch my p's and q's in public. Clearly I need to go back home and pray about all this and see what I should do to get the information I need.

RECONCILER   I think that is a good note on which to finish. I think that I am with Progressive here. We should stick to our specific agenda, work out a good plan of action, and then set about developing the political strategy to save United Methodism. Even though I am fearless about tackling controversial topics from the pulpit, this is not one I have really explored in any detail. Besides, it could well be a distraction from the main task. It is exactly the sort of thing that an unscrupulous opponent could use to discredit us and ruin our plans to save United Methodism. We have to save United Methodism. We need to keep our eye firmly on that ball. Perhaps we should strike that part of our conversation from the Minutes.

PIETIST   Now wait a minute! I have raised an entirely legitimate question. This is a round table, you know, where everybody gets to bring their ideas, and questions, and worries. Did I get that wrong?

RECONCILER   I really do have to go. I am already two minutes behind on my schedule for the day.

PROGRESSIVE   I am off to have a shower. I feel so soiled and unclean after this last exchange between us. I need a good bath to get over what I have just heard.

PIETIST   Maybe I should go back and have another conversation with Traditional and Evangelical. This will not be easy. Clearly, I need to pray about what I should do.

Dialogue V

Disagreement on who is splitting the Church

PIETIST   I hope you don't mind my getting in touch with you and initiating another round of conversation. The conversation with Progressive and Reconciler turned out to be much more difficult than I expected. I did not anticipate that Progressive would be quite so aggressive but I can only live by my own convictions and let others do what they will with them. I am glad there are no hard feelings on my change of mind and heart. From past experience and observation I know how tough my side of the house can be on its own troops. However, in the end one has to stand with the will of God and let things fall out as they will.

TRADITIONALIST   Well said. And I hope you realize how things are going to fall out if you and Reconciler win the day?

PIETIST   What do you mean?

TRADITIONALIST   You will have split United Methodism into two or three camps and done irreparable damage to the church. Is this what you want to do? We have had a very fragile unity over the last forty years and it can all too easily be scattered to the winds.

PIETIST   Absolutely not! I cannot even begin to imagine how you can make an accusation like that. It is Evangelical who wants to split the church and is working on plans to bring that about!

TRADITIONALIST   Consider an analogy. Suppose you were to belong to a political party that has had a particular identity and a set of practices that it has formally agreed on for forty years. These practices are not arbitrary and have been central to its identity from the beginning. This political party has vocal minorities which has aggressively opposed the practices. For those difficult forty years, however, the party has upheld those practices and shows no sign of changing those policies in the foreseeable future. Increasingly frustrated over the years, the minority presses home their agenda to the point where they become the majority in certain units of the party. They constantly try to undo the policies and related practices, set themselves apart by wearing a special dress code, refuse to implement the policies at crucial leverage points in the system, and so on. They then discover that if they team up with a self-identified moderate leader and his associates they can establish their minority opinion as a local option even though they know that the local option is a mere stepping stone to final victory. They also know that this option will mean that a host of those who are part of the majority will simply have to leave if they are to retain even the semblance of integrity. Yet they forge ahead regardless. Now who do you think is dividing the party? Is it the minority who has finally figured out a strategy to get their way? Or is it the group that has worked to preserve the long-standing policies and procedures of the party?

PIETIST   You are simply trying to trap me again with you either/or dualistic ways of thinking and I am not going to play that game.

TRADITIONALIST   So you are going to renounce all responsibilities for the obvious consequences of your actions at this point? Is this now what true piety means for you? I can see that you may not want to judge others. Well and good. But I find it astonishing that after all your talk about having had a spiritual and moral change of heart and mind you have now given yourself a free pass on evaluating the obvious knock-on effects of your current actions.

PIETIST   We are not splitting the church. We are simply trying to find a way forward to a better future.

TRADITIONALIST   Suppose a train driver knows that his faulty brakes are likely to cause a serious accident. He does not want to have an accident for there are likely to be casualties. Yet rather than deal with the faulty brakes he joins with others in going beyond the speed-limit and does further damage to the brakes. When the likely accident happens and there are serious casualties, can he walk away and pretend that he has no responsibility for the casualties?

PIETIST   I refuse to accept you analogy. I have never thought of our church as having faulty brakes. Brakes belong to bicycles, cars, and trains; they do not belong to churches.

TRADITIONALIST   You know as surely as the sun will come up tomorrow that if you win then you will be placing your former friends and colleagues in an impossible position. It will be the kind of position that you yourself were in when you were working through to a change of mind on gay marriage. You felt you had to go through with your decision and make it public even though you knew it would have all sorts of real consequences. You were also prepared in the name of obedience and faithfulness to stay the course. You stepped up and were ready to take responsibility for what would happen as a result of your change of mind.

PIETIST   When you put the issue that way I think I get what you are saying. I do realize that my actions have consequences for others. What you say makes me uncomfortable, but I still don't think it is fair to say that I am splitting the church. It is Evangelical who is splitting the church.

TRADITIONALIST   So you are prepared to judge poor old Evangelical, even though he refuses to accept your narrative of events which so conveniently lets you off the hook. You readily criticize him and his friends for being dualistic, hateful, hierarchical, dogmatic in his biblical interpretation, and a host of other bad things that you insist are destroying the beauty of the Bride of Christ. If we disagree with you on your agree-to-disagree policy you think we are dead wrong and need to get as spiritual as you are. Frankly, I find your self-righteous condemnation of those who disagree with you completely incoherent. It is all of a piece with your refusal to take responsibility for the consequences of your actions.

PIETIST   There you go again attacking me personally.

TRADITIONALIST   Read it that way if you like. In fact I am not attacking you personally. I am going after certain obvious vices, like, failing to take responsibility for one's actions. I am also condemning the practice of making a grand fuss about not judging others while all the while calling out those who disagree with you as wrong, hateful, dualistic, and heaven knows what else. This is a form of hidden dualism that you conveniently ignore. As a matter of fact I like you. If you were hit by a car I would be the first to drive you to the hospital. But I can clearly distinguish between my commitment to you as a person and the incoherent and implausible judgments you are asking me to accept. I can even believe that you could change your mind, painful though that might be.

PIETIST   I suppose you will now berate me with the old slogan that we should love the sinner and hate the sin. That too is part of your dualistic way of thinking. We have seen that one played out again in the debate about homosexual practice. What you are saying, whether you like it or not, is a direct attack on me. That is what I expect from people like you and my Lord tells me to bear it as best I can.

TRADITIONALIST   It was the Lord who taught the principle that we should distinguish the sin from the sinner. I recall that when he protected a woman who was going to be stoned for adultery that he told her to go and sin no more. So I would have thought that your theology would have picked this up along the way. To be honest, I see little hope of this line of investigation going anywhere. Does piety now also mean we have to send our brains on a holiday and ignore well tested moral principles, like, love the sinner but do not condone the sin?

PIETIST   There you go again; you have turned this into a trial, into a grand investigation. I think it is time to change the subject. I trust we can agree that we are now going round in circles. Let me try another angle that might help you understand how I see things. As you know I was brought up in the conservative wing of United Methodism and have served my whole ministry in that world. It is a world that I know intimately. I was generally known as an evangelical. As you well know that is not a static world.

If you take it across the last four hundred years it has changed in all sorts of ways and yet remained recognizably evangelical. Within it even today, there are all sorts of disagreements. This is nothing new. What is emerging across United Methodism is that people like me are remaining orthodox in doctrine and spirituality but we are evolving in our position on gay marriage. They are orthodox on doctrine and progressive on social issues. There are far more of us out there than you realize. We once took a conservative position; we no longer find it plausible. This is why Reconciler's proposal has struck such a chord so quickly with so many. The process of change is not easy to describe formally but change is what it is. Partly it is a matter of not liking the hardline attitudes of so many conservatives. Partly it is a matter of encountering faithful gay folk who want the same respect and rights of straight folk. We need not rehearse arguments that are so shopworn that it would be tedious to go over them again. I suppose a watershed factor was the realization that there are differences of opinion on how to handle the relevant biblical texts. Once I came to see that the so-called progressive option was compatible with the Bible, it was easy to make the transition. If the Bible is silent on the issue then I think our church should be silent on it as well. It hit me in the end with the force of a divine revelation and I could no longer be silent.

TRADITIONALIST   We are going back round again to that endless merry-go-round of personal divine revelation and biblical interpretation.

Innovation and Postmodernity within Evangelicalism

PIETIST   Actually I do not want us to be side-tracked. My main point here is that the world of evangelicalism is changing and has been doing so for at least the last decade. In his own way Reconciler is the poster child for what has been happening. He has run up a flag and you will be astonished at the names of prominent evangelical pastors that show up to salute it. Think of that group that goes under the name of emergent. Think of the innovations that we have seen in worship. Think of the new waves in evangelical biblical scholarship. Think of the many evangelicals who no longer believe in the existence of the soul after their careful study of recent neuroscience. Think of the move by some evangelicals to develop a Protestant doctrine of purgatory. Think of the network of evangelicals who have come out in favor of the Affordable Care Act. They have shifted on a whole host of theological and moral positions that were once thought orthodox and unchangeable. I am just one of many that have changed. I have no doubt there will be many more who will come on board with support for Reconciler. They have not for one moment ceased to be Biblical. They have simply come to a different interpretation of the Bible. United Methodism has always been a biblical denomination. We have worked out what to do in the past when we disagreed on what the Bible means for our theology and ethics. This is exactly what we need to do now. We should sit down around a round table and ask the good Lord to help us figure out how to agree to disagree.

TRADITIONALIST   I think you are right on the facts here. I once was told that evangelicals were fundamentalists with good manners. It was a clever comment but hopelessly inaccurate, of course, for the reasons you specify. Progressive, I suspect, would dismiss them all as literalists who really think that the Bible was dictated by God. There is a popular myth abroad that they are a monolithic group that has never changed and will never change. We need not go into all the highways and byways of history at this stage. It would only distract us further. I also agree that Reconciler is banking on winning over the evolving evangelical leaders of United Methodism. If he can crack that group he may well win.

EVANGELICAL   I have also given serious thought to this development. I also have a theory of why we are faced with this potential shift within the evangelical camp. The bottom line is that many evangelicals have been seduced by the sirens of post-modernity. They have unwittingly caved to a disastrous accommodation to the view that there is no truth at all or that all truth is relative. In the process they have taken that first step away from the truth of the Bible that in time will lead to a complete reconstruction of the Christian faith. Deep down they have already abandoned any serious doctrine of biblical authority. They have no objective standard of theology or morality at the end of the day. We are left with personal opinions or interest group opinions. They write learned articles embracing with delight that ultimately their own scholarship is subjective rather than objective. It is a neat way of winning prizes for their work; but the prizes are worthless because everyone gets the prize they covet in the end.

PIETIST   You are now drawing me into a whole new world even though I think more can be said in its favor than you would allow. Clearly you did not hear what I just said a moment ago about my commitment to biblical authority. I believe in the Bible as much as you do! You think you have distilled its truth objectively once and for all, but you cannot be serious. There are many interpretations of what the Bible says. You know that fact as well as I do; 'subjective' may not be the right word but it is certainly somewhere in that neighborhood rather in the neighborhood identified as 'objective'.

EVANGELICAL   Of course, I accept that there are many interpretations. However, you exaggerate the extent of those disagreements. One of the tragedies of our situation is that we have given up trying to persuade each other on the basis of real exegesis and moved the whole debate to the platitude that we cannot agree on scripture. The Reformers would never have agreed to that; nor would John Wesley. Things have gotten worse with the arrival of postmodernity where everything gets reduced to interests, preferences, social location, and the like. Of course, once you move to this level we are supposed to take these claims to be objectively accurate. I read one blog recently that we urged the adoption of a much more inclusive approach to reading scripture. We need to have gays at the table now, it was claimed. Check things out and you will be able to take a course on Queer interpretation of scripture at many of our seminaries. Do you imagine for one moment that this will enable us to read scripture together at your round table and have anything other than chaos? You can add prayer meetings round the clock for seven days a week and we will not make any progress.

PIETIST   We certainly haven't tried that option last time I checked!

On Prayer and Postmodernity

EVANGELICAL   And do you think for one moment that we would find a way to pray together that would last for more than five minutes? Think of the disputes that would immediately arise. We would have to sort out who is invited to the table, who gets to sit at the highest chair, who gets to set the hours of prayer, which prayers may or not be included, whether or not we can address God as Father, whether we should pray in the name of Jesus, and who gets to pronounce the benediction if there is one. Think of how difficult it is to organize worship at our Annual Conferences. The first and last question is not about God but is always about ourselves. How well are I and my group represented? Who gets to sit at the highest table? Who speaks and for how long? Who represents who? Who has harmed who by what has been said? What group has been excluded? We now have stewards to keep tabs on who speaks and for how long. At times I think we are really sailing close to idolatry; we and our group matter more than God when it comes to our worship together. Maybe we should be honest and simply say that much of our worship really is idolatry.

PIETIST   You are ignoring two crucial points. First, we have a round table, so there could not be a dispute about who get the highest chair. The chairs are all the same height. Second, you are discounting the presence of the Holy Spirit. The Spirit will take care of all this. We will be patient and work our way through these questions.

EVANGELICAL   Actually, you never said that the chairs all had to be the same height, so until that is further specified and agreed on we cannot even get started. I leave that aside, however, for I am sure you have already figured that out from past experience. The more important point is this. You are simply using the Holy Spirit as a labor-saving device to evade the real problems you have to face. Who is this Holy Spirit? Do we spell it with a small or a capital S? What gender should we ascribe to the Spirit? Are we going to have prophecies in tongues and the interpretation of tongues? Is the Spirit going to give us all the new revelation that you claim to have heard? Is the Bible to be used to settle these issues? What do we do when we disagree on what the Bible says around your round table? We are right back where we started.

PIETIST   You are obviously operating out of a heart of fear and distrust. I am operating out of a heart of peace and trust.

EVANGELICAL   Oh! I see, you are the good guy and I am the bad guy. So much for the end of dualistic thinking!

PIETIST   Stop twisting my words and judging me! Come back down to holy reality and hear me out. The other claim you make is that we do not believe in truth; essentially, you claim that we are relativists on moral issues. This is the nub of your comments about living in a postmodern church. This is an easy objection to answer. If we were as you describe us then why do you think we are so passionate about what we believe and about why we must change the harmful language and oppressive practices of our church? We think that we are morally right in changing our minds. We are objectivists in our moral vision. So you are misrepresenting our position. We may believe that modernity is over and done with, together with the old forms of liberal Protestantism that are now barely kicking. So in that sense we may be heard to say that we live in a postmodern world. What else should we call the new world we inhabit? After modernity comes postmodernity; that is a natural and apt way to describe the transition from one period in history to another. But you are dead wrong about how we think about theology and morality. We are objectivists who think that there is a correct view about sexual practice. As you know by now, we think that you are objectively wrong about it.

EVANGELICAL   You are not out of the woods just yet. You also hold that The United Methodist Church should as a church agree to disagree. The church cannot come up with an objectively correct view about sexual morality. This affords a better way to press home my postmodern description of your position. Think of it like this. You have your my opinion, I have mine.

This conference will be conservative; that one over there will be progressive or discerning. This local church will go this way; the one down the street will go another way. Given that we cannot agree on the truth of the matter we will negotiate our way into the future. This is precisely what a postmodern church will be; it will have no objective resolution to the most important moral debate that has arisen in the recent history of the church; the resolution will be relative to the way local Annual Conferences and local churches divide over the issue. This is simply a version of personal preferences when you look below the surface. That's in part what I mean when I claim that you have accommodated to the culture. You end up with diverse communities of local preferences and do all you can to make a virtue out of necessity.

PIETIST   There is truth here but it is not the whole truth. You conveniently forget that each community that would emerge on the other side of our proposal would be able to stand by its own convictions about what is objectively the case. You can enact your conviction about what is objectively the case; others can then enact what they think is objectively the case. So we are not giving up on truth or objectivity; we are seeking to preserve unity whereas you want to plan for disunity and division. We are in fact securing unity by insisting on our diversity. We are the reconcilers; you are the dividers. We are giving you all that any person of good will could reasonably desire or demand. The only way I can explain your resistance is that you are in denial and are reaching for some kind of fancy philosophical theory with which to badger us. I would take this one step further. For years you have been threatening to split the church. I did this myself, but only in private for to do that in public would mean a lynching at General Conference. I saw what happened to Bill Hinson of First Church, Houston, at the General Conference when he tried to get it onto the edge of the table and was left high and dry by the progressives who seemed initially to support him. Some folk I know personally honestly believe that this may have been a factor in his early death. On the surface you deny that you are making threats. The truth is that this time around you are really taking the threat of splitting to a whole new level. We have had enough of your threats. This is no way to behave in the household of God. Your threats are now out in the open for all to see. We are now calling your bluff on it by offering a third way that exposes you for what you really are. You are a reactionary conservative evangelical who at bottom is a divider and a splitter.

EVANGELICAL   That is a clever change of subject you make at the end. You have now abandoned both reason and good will. Note the innuendo in that last comment. You are now implicitly claiming that we have two camps of evangelicals, the conservative evangelicals and the progressive evangelicals. A distinction along these lines has been surfacing from time to time and stating it openly deserves serious attention. I have tended to think evangelicals would stick together and that we could weather the storms if we remained as one group. Note also your clever and devious way of depicting what is going on. It is ridiculous that folk who identify the conditions under which they cannot stay within United Methodism are now charged with making threats that if they do not get their way they will split the church or leave the church. If someone honestly identifies the conditions under which they could no longer be a member, say, of a political party that is surely a matter for transparency and honesty. When something similar happens in the church, you then seize on it and turn it into a threat. So much for all your talk about not misrepresenting others in your honest dialogue! You take what is a very painful and even agonizing statement of where we are and immediately use it as a weapon against us. We know the game that is being played here and we are not going to be fooled by it for one moment.

Division within the Evangelical Household

TRADITIONALIST   I think that Pietist has hit upon something of the great significance in our conversation. Evangelicalism within United Methodism is coming apart at the joints. There is a further division happening right under our noses that we have been ignoring.

PIETIST   I suppose you will now accuse me of that division as well!

TRADITIONALIST   This is a division that you illustrate rather than help bring about. Let me try and explain your unhappy discovery. This particular division has happened in part because evangelicalism is an unstable coalition of interests that will disintegrate if there is nothing more to hold it together. It is an inherently unstable experiment in modern Christianity that will not survive intact unless other elements are present in the life of the church.

EVANGELICAL   Like the great canonical faith of the church?

TRADITIONALIST   Yes indeed. Thomas Oden and the Confessing Movement did what they could to drum that into our heads. That Fighting Irishman who was sent to Texas because he had so many sins lent a hand in that operation as well. He knew that he would pay a high price for challenging the shoddy scholarship that so annoyed him. In many ways and at great odds those folk have been incredibly successful in upgrading the core commitments of evangelicals within United Methodism. There are other factors that are potential sources of division within the evangelical camp that you and I can discuss at our leisure. I am thinking of in-house differences on how best to state the doctrine of scripture, how best to relate scripture to the great faith of the church, and the very status of claims about the Bible in the early church, in historic Methodism, and in the modern period. It would be a fatal mistake if we were to allow our potential disagreements in those domains to prevent us from standing together in the crisis that we face right now in the church. We desperately need the big tent you mentioned earlier. We are facing the end of Methodism not just as we know it but as a tradition we love and cherish.

PIETIST   I fail to see why you think that division within evangelicalism is such a big deal.

TRADITIONALIST   Here is why. Up until now there has been a firm coalition between evangelicals, a lot of centrists, and folk outside the continental USA, that has held firm. Once the evangelicals divide then we are at sea on where things may fall out at the next General Conference. This is what gives Evangelical heartburn late at night. The more politically astute units in the progressive camp cannot believe their good luck. They believe that the opposition has cracked right down the middle. Reconciler has not just exposed the fault line; he has opened up what has been tried again and again and failed, namely, some version of the local option. Progressives no longer have to carry the can; they realize that Reconciler along with the Hamiltonians and Slaughterites and their progressive evangelical associates will carry the can for them. This is a total godsend, a gift that has been dropped from heaven out of the blue, a free ticket to the Promised Land. A mere shift of about five percent of the vote is all they need if you look at the statistics. As these developments take their course we are in the process of digging the grave of United Methodism once and for all.

EVANGELICAL   I think you are exaggerating the potential support for Reconciler at this point. Certainly we need to count the votes as best we can but I am skeptical about the number of progressive evangelicals who are out there. A handful of prominent pastors who have shifted their ground is all that exists at the moment; and I am not sure how firm they are in their commitments; some of them have not really begun to think through what is at stake. Who knows maybe even Pietist will have second thoughts. The debate has only begun in earnest in the church as a whole. Most folk on the ground have no idea what is going on in the courts of the church. We have a long way to go.

PIETIST   It is certainly nice to be given the space to think for myself for a change!

EVANGELICAL   Paul was happy to welcome back Peter after his lapse of judgment and legend has it they established a thriving new Christian community in Rome. So who knows what the future may hold. Who knows what the Spirit may yet do to give us all a second chance to get out of this mess and develop a thriving future for Methodism. Whatever we do we must keep the channels open between the various interest groups that exist. It is only natural that in times of crises folk go out on limbs that break under the strain. We really do need to be ready to welcome one another and help one another when that happens. Personal conversations and small informal group meetings are crucial in making this happen.

PIETIST   Now you are beginning to speak my language!

TRADITIONALIST   Before you too wander off into the future, do you mind, Pietist, if I concentrate for a stretch on a conversation with Evangelical.

PIETIST   Go ahead. Let's take a short break first. I assume I can add my two cents worth if I so desire.

EVANGELICAL   Of course.

Dialogue VI

Traditionalist Goes Apocalyptic

EVANGELICAL   I am glad we took a break for you were really beginning to sound apocalyptic. It is utterly premature to speak of the death of United Methodism, as if the whole world was coming to an end. That's what I can hear my yellow-dog Democrat barber saying. She is a Southern Baptist who has long been separated from her husband. When I brought up what was happening in our church this morning she said, tongue in check, "Jesus needs to come back and usher in the End."

TRADITIONALIST   I am not getting into that hornet's nest.

EVANGELICAL   Good. But given what you are saying you should surely accept that we need a strategy that will do exactly what you care about, that is, preserve a robust vision of Methodism as a national and global expression of the church for the future.

TRADITIONALIST   I am not even sure that this is possible any more. We will be fortunate if we can keep alive a fragmented version of the faith that will be available when the current trends bottom out and there just might be a return to the faith once delivered to the saints.

EVANGELICAL   You are really beginning to think that this is the case?

TRADITIONALIST   Yes, indeed. We really need a short-term and a long-term vision. In the short term I think United Methodism is finished. We will dig our own grave at the next General Conference. Even if we end up with deadlock and we survive on paper, we will be mere bits and pieces. We will still exist but there will not be a United Methodism that is in any way united. We have now gotten to the point where everyone is going to be a loser. The progressives will be the least affected because they are determined to win at any cost to the connection; and frankly most of them are so myopic they do not care. If Reconciler turns out to represent the middle, or if the middle follows him and his team, they will soon reach a point of no return. It will be like the early days in trans-Atlantic aviation. Airplanes only had so much fuel on board. Once they reached a certain point in the journey, a red light came on in the dashboard; once that happened, they knew they could not turn back. Mark my words. There will be no option of a retreat back into the status quo with dignity. There will be no way to save face. It would take a corporate miracle to put Humpty Dumpty back together again. While I believe in miracles, I am very skeptical about corporate miracles. Right now I see no way back to the table, given the turn of events over the last six months. The water has been spilt and it cannot be gathered up again.

EVANGELICAL   This really is scary talk!

TRADITIONALIST   To be sure, there will be all sorts of polite noises about appreciating how much we value the contribution made to the life of the church. There will be pious blarney about how ready everybody is to listen and thus advance the discussion in a charitable manner. United Methodists are great at larding the opening and closing remarks with expressions of civility. This is certainly an advance on a verbal shoot-out from the get-go. Do not be fooled, we are in a fight to the death, and all sides are sure it is not going to be their death. Perhaps you are the exception here.

EVANGELICAL   You have read my sentiments exactly.

TRADITIONALIST   Let me get speculative for a moment. Take the numbers. If we divide amicably, or rather, if we divide acrimoniously, you can be sure that any projections offered will be hopelessly inflated, just as our numbers are now. Take eight million as a round figure. By the time all this is over when you add up the numbers I bet a good bottle of Australian wine that we will have half the numbers we now have. Many members in our local churches will take this as a time to stop going to church altogether or they will move quietly to another denomination. Take our seminaries, colleges, and universities. They will be thrown up in the air with most of them opting for independence. Some will almost certainly go out of business. Our Boards and Agencies will be decimated. The Publishing House will continue its downward spiral into a marginal outfit, desperate to find the bestselling pastors and authors who will keep it afloat. Pensions will be preserved because the crowbar of personal interest will keep it buoyant. By way of contrast, take the pastors who are in the latter half of their career. Many will stay in place until they can retire and get out. The middle group who are now being royally shafted because of the policy of betting the store on younger folk reaching a new generation will have even lower morale than they currently have. The younger generation will scatter like sheep on the hill.

EVANGELICAL   I confess there are moments when I have nightmares along exactly these lines.

TRADITIONALIST   These are not nightmares; they are the realities that are now staring us all in the face. You may continue to hope for the best, but I prefer to prepare for the worst.

EVANGELICAL   That is exactly why we are not prepared to take separation off the table. In a way separation is a doomsday scenario. We will do all we can to make it amicable, but it takes two to tango. We have calculated for better or worse that your option will never work. We have no real interest in pursuing it. We are well aware that various groups will be working on this; they are not going to go quietly into the night. We prefer to skip that intervening step of trying one more time to fix the loopholes in the *Book of Discipline*. Fix one set of loopholes and they will create others. Besides, we are not going to waste any more time or energy on this. We are done with standing in the way of others who have come to radically different conclusions than us. I hope the opposition will be as magnanimous and charitable as we intend to be. Our energy will be focused on getting folk to see that we really are at a fork in the road. This will require patience on our part. I know there are some who have had enough and would jump ship tomorrow if they could. But even they understand that people need time to think things through and come to a settled conviction on what needs to be done. The current talk about United Methodism splitting at the next General Conference is very wide of the mark. Change in our system takes time. Our ancestors built caution and reserve into the structures so that there would be no hasty or impetuous decisions that we would come to regret later. We fully agree with this wisdom. We will take this journey one step at a time. We differ from you in making sure that we have all options on the table.

TRADITIONALIST   We need not rehearse that disagreement all over again. Now here is the good news. These days will pass. Not in my lifetime or yours; but in the long run, they will pass. At some point the bottom will fall out of the alternatives currently being patched together as a unified front. When that happens we will need successors in the wings to help as best they can. What is at stake is a viable legacy in the long-run. The current generation does not have a monopoly on truth or morality. It is the height of absurdity when folk barely out of university or seminary suddenly become the experts on what Wesley was all about and lecture us on what he stood for. They have not even taken the trouble to read his canonical sermons, much less understand them. I am all for teaching and encouraging the young (it is one of my lifelong passions), but it is ridiculous when their initial judgments and impulsive sentiments are suddenly offered up as a reason for the church to get with their program. Some of them will one day grow up and be mugged by reality. Some of them will take their delusional self-righteousness to the grave. Some of them, when they think it through, may well be converted. Many more than you think are exceptionally intelligent and will stand by the faith of the church.

EVANGELICAL   I get it hard to resist the hard realism of your observations.

TRADITIONALIST   To be sure, you and I have different ways of framing the central issues. We may haggle over what is primary and secondary, about how to frame the debate, and about how to best to state our case. However, we both know that while the vote will be on sexual morality, there are other equally important issues at stake. We did not put that topic on the table; others did and then have the nerve to say that we are obsessed about sex. The other big fish being fried include the upholding the traditional faith of the church, winning souls to the great God and Savior of the Gospel, preserving holiness, loving the socks off our neighbors, standing by the knowledge given in divine revelation, and preserving the deep insights given to us in our fragile and very human United Methodist tradition. Our opponents do not believe this about us. That is their problem not ours. We need to stand by the light we have received and let God vindicate us. I think that Pietist can really understand this element in our stance. In the end I have much more fear of the judgment of God that I do of the judgments of those who daily misrepresent our intentions and have no real interest in engaging with our concerns beyond shoring up the political agenda now in play. They have the nerve to tell us what we will gain from their half-way houses and stop-gap arrangements. The lecture us on platitudes about our families and how we should be reasonable and accept the complex local option they are busily constructing. We have our own judgments about such matters and until we are convinced otherwise we will stay the course. Rest assured we are not alone when you look across the face of Christianity in the contemporary world.

EVANGELICAL   I certainly agree with you on that last point. And you are right about the more general point that we have different angles of vision at times. You see the glass empty; I see it as at least half full. Even within United Methodism I think there are a lot of people who are prepared to break. Some will even consider walking away from their buildings and letting the Annual Conference pick up the mortgage. They are fed up with the tactics of the progressives. They are tired going to Annual Conferences and other meetings to fight the same battle over and over again. They have no intention of spending the rest of their days talking about sex much less gay sex. They want to get on with the work of the Lord. They are utterly opposed to the wider agenda of progressives; that agenda is hopelessly thin theologically and spiritually and in the long-run it has no future. They are also fed up with decline. They know how to grow churches. They love Wesley and the tradition that stems from him. They will want their brothers and sisters outside the United States to go with them. Even some of our bishops see the writing on the wall and will gladly come with us. Indeed some of us are beginning to imagine a whole new vision for United Methodism and other Wesleyan bodies. If we have time I would love to pursue this in another session. In the meantime we have our hands full. I can assure you, as we look at the option of separation, we are not going to do this either half-heartedly or by half-measures. We will get out there and make our case and it will be as smart and professional as we can make it. We will be patient and take as long as it takes to achieve our goals.

TRADITIONALIST   I would be delighted to hear what you have in mind.

EVANGELICAL   It sounds as if you are open to the kind of vision that could well be central to our future as Methodists. Working this out will be a stretch for some of our people but keep thinking about it. I want you to lend a hand in thinking through what is needed to get things moving. We need all hands on deck. In the meantime be prepared for all sorts of opposition. You can be sure that there will be backroom work of desperate leaders who will be ready to shut us all down in a deadlock, just as they do in Congress. If the whole show is going to go up in smoke, they will stop everything in its tracks and send everybody home to lick their wounds from the next General Conference. Somebody will know how to do this through the Judicial Council or a clever resolution that will squeeze through by two votes. We need to be ready for such an unwelcome outcome. Hard though it would be we need to recall the old adage of Wesley, the best of all is God is with us. Or as some now prefer to say: God is good, all the time!

PIETIST   All the time, God is with us!

TRADITIONALIST   So you, Pietist, might change your mind. You would be like those Calvinists in early Methodism whom Wesley was delighted to welcome so long as they did not disrupt the work as a whole by agitating for their position within Methodism and systematically disrupting its central work and ministry. You might even squeeze back into the big tent! I bet you underestimate how readily many conservatives would take you back into the fold. They have been brutal in the past with some of their wayward children, but they are not as heartless as you think or may have seen for yourself. In times like this we all understand that all sorts of surprising stuff can come out of the woodwork. There are deep friendships below the surface here that can cover a lot of missteps and false starts. Providence is ingenious at weaving secret straight lines through the broken pathways of humanity. This time around we can see that Evangelical is in no hurry to come to a quick and easy vision of how best to proceed. He is clear about the big picture and the broad principles that will govern his actions but there is lots of flexibility in some of the details.

On Love, Law, and Unity

PIETIST   Not so fast, my good friend. There are lots of other issues to discuss before I would even begin to consider a change of mind. Let me pick up two of them. Where is love in the midst of all you doomsday scenario? Moreover, I notice that nowhere have you said a word about the unity of the church. So where do you stand on that? Do you even care about the unity of the church? How do you understand the mandate to pursue the unity of the church?

TRADITIONALIST   On the issue of love, the answer is simple. There is no question of not loving all and sundry, including our enemies. Long ago I welcomed Wesley's slogan that we were the friends of all and the enemies of none. We are required to love as a matter of obedience. And if we love Christ we will keep his commandments. Equally, love and obedience show up in the debate about homosexuality. Both Reconciler and I agree that there are standards, mandates, rules, norms, imperatives, and the like. I think you also agree because you obeyed what you thought you heard the Spirit say to you. So any move to set love against law or against obedience will not get to first base. Wesley too was patently clear about this as his sermons on antinomianism and his love for the epistle of James make clear. So I hope we can put this topic to bed immediately. Playing love against law and obedience is as old as the Fall and we are not going to fall for that again.

PIETIST   And the challenge you and Evangelical pose to the unity of the church? What about that?

TRADITIONALIST   You mean the challenge that you, Progressive and Reconciler, now pose to the unity of the church?

PIETIST   Alright, let me go back to one of my more neutral question. How do you understand the mandate to pursue the unity of the church?

TRADITIONALIST   I totally accept that mandate, as years of formal and informal service in the ecumenical work of The United Methodist Church attest. Now let me cut to the chase. There is no chance of covering all the bases on how I conceive unity or on how I think unity is secured and preserved. Suffice it to say this. Unity cannot be secured without adequate instruments of unity. The agent of unity is the Holy Spirit. However, the Holy Spirit from the beginning has deployed a host of instruments and agencies to secure unity in the church. One crucial instrument, for example, was the Apostolic Council of Acts 15. This was the model both for the great ecumenical councils of the church and for our own Annual and General Conferences. The Holy Spirit inspired the church to invent such gatherings where contested issues that inevitably arise could be aired and worked through to a resolution. Here is the payoff of this observation. It is exactly this instrument of unity that is now at risk because of the behavior of you and your new associates. We all have seen what has been happening at our General Conferences. They are now descending into a farce. That is the relevant and crucial point that needs to be made in any conversation about unity at this point in time. The first step towards any serious vision of unity is that we restore confidence in the procedures of our General Conference.

PIETIST   We may well be on the same page here. If you read my proposal carefully you can see that I am suggesting something along these lines when I spell out what is at stake in gathering around my round table.

TRADITIONALIST   It may look as if we are on the same page, but the truth is otherwise. For one thing, you are not really appealing to the same kind of instrument of unity, for your whole approach is predicated on a personal divine revelation that gives a special privilege to your seat at the table. Think of it as a special lamp that is above your head while the rest of us have to make do with the general light of nature and the light of Christ. More importantly, your whole approach assumes that we have not had the guidance of the Holy Spirit over the last forty years when we have gathered in General Conference and worked over the issues again and again. You set aside the deliberations of General Conference and then want to set up your own special conference and start all over again. You are either a functional atheist at this point, or you have come to the conclusion that the Holy Spirit declined our invitation to be present. Then to crown it all, you expect us to accept the outcome of your special conference as supplying a Word from God or inspired guidance. Do you really expect us to have any confidence in this process when you set aside the deliberations of the only instrument of unity that we have had to date? This whole way of thinking is self-referentially incoherent. Your proposal is predicated on both the rejection and the acceptance of conferencing as a place of guidance and as an instrument of unity. Aside from the difficulties I laid out earlier, this is the deep reason why I shall not be showing up at your round table.

PIETIST   I am really sorry you feel this way. You will be in my prayers.

TRADITIONALIST   Maybe you should redirect your prayers back towards yourself. Have you begun to think of the impact your proposal will have on our ecumenical relations? Can't you see that you are effectively killing off any serious engagement with our Roman Catholic and Orthodox partners in ecumenical dialogue? I do not what to pursue this further at this point, but we have already seen the response of the Orthodox leadership in Russia to developments in the Anglican Communion. They have simply given up on any future conversations with Anglicans. The consequences of what you are proposing are catastrophic for our past ecumenical aspirations. In reality you are condemning United Methodism to a future as a dying mainline Protestant sect. I know you can postpone the consequences in the short-term, for the whole ecumenical agenda has to be rethought from the bottom up; however, I want to keep our ecumenical options alive. You have just buried any serious ecumenical future for us as United Methodists. This is just one more instance of your refusal to take responsibility for the consequences for your action.

PIETIST   I confess that as an evangelical I was at best luke-warm about ecumenism. However, I can see your point. The great middle of our church was enthusiastic about ecumenism; it was a major plank in their agenda; I think you are right that they will have to face the fall-out if they go with me and Reconciler. Given that ecumenism is now pretty much brain dead, I doubt if this will be a major problem for them.

TRADITIONALIST   In fact your third way exemplifies disunity in ways I suspect you do not realize at this point. It is not easy to work out exactly what constitutes unity in the church. However, when outsiders look in they will be amazed to see what will happen if you stay the course with Reconciler. If they see common liturgies, interchangeable ministries, common teaching, and common canon law, they will be able to see one united body. However, this is not what they will see for each group will have to work up its own version of these crucial signs and instruments of unity. This is not unity; it is diversity masquerading as unity. It fits with the claim that in actual fact we are already deeply divided. This is one reason why Evangelical refuses to say that he is dividing the church. He insists that he is just acknowledging a reality that already exists and facing up to the facts that are staring us in the face.

PIETIST   I take you point and will mull it over with some care in the future.

Another Summation, and a Footnote

EVANGELICAL   Let me see if I can begin to summarize where we are. I doubt if we have made much progress with Pietist beyond some generally accepted platitudes that we all love our church, that we believe there are standards of morality that any church should identify and uphold as the times dictate, that we recognize the gravity of situation, and that there is now a significant split in the evangelical camp. We also agree that appeals to scripture and to divine revelation are essential in the debate, that reference to postmodern trends in our culture are relevant, and that we need the presence of the Holy Spirit in our public assemblies. Finally, we are all committed to the exercise of comprehensive love, to unity, and to an honest exchange of views.

PIETIST AND TRADITIONALIST *in unison*   We are on board on all of this.

EVANGELICAL   I think it fair to say that Traditionalist and I agree on the gravity of the situation. We both believe that the house is on fire. We think that the fallout given current developments and trends is potentially catastrophic. At the very least we would like Pietist and his associates to take responsibility for exacerbating a division within the church which is now in danger of becoming explicit and institutional. We agree that we stand unapologetically for the great faith of the church across the centuries. We agree that the agreement to disagree is a covert way to change the teaching of the church so that it endorses same-sex marriages in a way that clearly fits with the Pietist's and Reconciler's recent adoption of the progressive agenda on this and related issues. This is not a neutral third way of the sort portrayed in the advertising; it is a partisan commitment that will have deep repercussions across the church globally. We agree that we should work together in the future and that if this is to be successful we will need to construct a big tent that will leave room for genuine differences. While we are open to informal conversations with those who disagree with us, we believe that another round of so-called holy conferencing, summits, and other assorted meetings, are a waste of time. They are effectively stalling tactics. The time for decision is now.

TRADITIONALIST   And how would you state the disagreements?

EVANGELICAL   We disagree on matters of style. Traditionalist thinks the time has come for much more militant forms of expression than I am. Traditionalist is also much more pessimistic about finding a way forward and is much more determined to get back in the trenches and shore up canon law. Traditionalist is more skeptical about the general health of the evangelical tradition than I am. I am more confident in persuading our opponents on the merits of our case from scripture than Traditionalist is. I am also more prepared to offer an olive branch. Traditionalist thinks that the time for olive branches is over; we need to call the fire brigade and put out the fire. He also thinks that I underestimate the animus that is in play against us; on his account we are on a hiding to nothing no matter how good our charitable intentions. At this point I am prepared to look at and think through a plan of separation. Traditionalist might allow this option as a last resort but has grave reservations as to whether it can succeed in practice.

TRADITIONALIST   Permit a final word on the fine summary of the situation. I am not sure if you would disagree with me in what follows but let me say it anyhow. If separation happens then you will have to be ready for the potential fall out on the conservative side. I do not mean here that there will be a general tendency in the air to divide again down the road, likely though that is. I think that we need to start naming the actual issues that could prove very difficult to resolve. Imagine that first called meeting, say, in a hotel in Atlanta. From one corner we hear a call for the introduction of term limits for bishops. Bishops, it will be said, are the real cause of our trouble and we need to take immediate action to clip their wings. From another corner we hear that it is time to rescind the decision to ordain women, for this is unbiblical, and it was this decision that was really the first step towards our current troubles around the ordination of practicing gays. From another we hear a motion to bar married divorcees from ordained ministry. We should never have allowed remarriage after divorce, it is argued, for this clearly contradicts the teaching of scripture and opened the flood gates to gay ordination. From another we are called upon to limit baptism to those who have personally accepted Christ, for we now operate in a post-Christian situation where infant baptism is no longer working. From the middle of the room someone insists that our doctrinal position must begin with a clear declaration that we are committed to a vision of scripture as the infallible Word of God. All our problems really go back, it is said, to this basic flaw within United Methodism, so we must move immediately to fix it. I have, in fact, my own thoughts on how we might deal with these potential crossroads. However, it is Evangelical who really needs to tell us what should be done at this point. These may not be included in your plans for General Conference but they will have to be taken up somewhere by somebody if we end up needing to pull the trigger on that nuclear strike option of yours.

EVANGELICAL   Rest assured we are fully aware of this danger but given what we have been through over the last thirty years I think you are exaggerating what we would face. It will be such a relief to go to meetings where we can stand on our own feet without having to walk around on egg shells. We are back again at how we see things: you are back looking at the half-empty glass; I see it more than half-full. I am absolutely sure that we can come together and move forward together. It will be a whole new day. I have one other piece of unfinished business. I am not sure we have yet nailed really accurately why it is that we cannot go along with Reconciler and Pietist on the third way. Could we try a summary of what is at stake? What makes our case so difficult is the subtle way in which the issue gets framed by those who claim to present a fresh way to resolve the conflict and to reach a more nuanced account of church teaching on marriage.

TRADITIONALIST   You are exactly right. I need a short break to gather my thoughts together and see what I can come up with. Before we get to that I think it would be good if we could have a sense of what might happen up ahead. We do not have a crystal ball but it is useful to have some sense of what the immediate future may bring forth. Maybe you should take the lead on this.

EVANGELICAL   Sure. Before that I will need a shot of good coffee.

TRADITIONALIST   I need a glass of good Australian wine!

Dialogue VII

Possible Options

EVANGELICAL   It was suggested that I get the ball rolling on what we are likely to face at the next General Conference and beyond.

TRADITIONALIST   I suspect that the options are pretty clear. I wish we could be as clear as to which one will pan out! It may well be that nothing will change. No group manages to score any significant victory in securing change in one way rather than another. Conservatives continue to hold the line and revisionists continue the effort to get things to reflect what they want. Everyone goes home pretty miserable but the more cheerful take comfort that a bloodbath was avoided. Most of the bishops are just happy to go home and take a break.

EVANGELICAL   This sounds like deadlock to me! However, let's begin with an option that fits with your general stance. In this instance we continue as we are, fix the loopholes in the *Book of Discipline*, strengthen the current position of the church on human sexuality, and make it possible for local progressive churches to leave with their property but without any assets above the level of the local church. Let's call this the enhanced status quo option.

TRADITIONALIST   This comes pretty close to what I would like to happen.

EVANGELICAL   A second option is that some variation of the third way gets adopted. The church continues with a default position in favor of the current teaching and practice but allows Annual Conferences and local congregations to opt out. We might see this as a case where there is a majority report and a minority report, but with this crucial difference. The minority is permitted to enact its own position in the life of the church.

Presumably, we would have to describe our stance in something like the following terms: The United Methodist Church holds to traditional teaching and practice on sexual practice but allows for dissenting practice under certain carefully delineated conditions. I am not sure this would capture what the third way would look like, but I think it comes close.

TRADITIONALIST   It will certainly do for now. I will pick up what I think of this stance later when it comes to my turn to carry the can.

EVANGELICAL   The third option would be to begin the process of exploring some kind of division. I notice that folk quickly assume a lot at this point when this option comes up. Many assume, for example, that division would be adopted at the next General Conference in 2016. Others assume that we would be looking at essentially three new bodies emerging on the other side of the dissolution of the current United Methodist Church. I see no reason to accept these assumptions; they simply reflect how fear kicks in and makes folk jump to conclusions. Let me try and keep it tight. Think of an option where we would pass a resolution appointing a Commission to develop a plan of separation that would be brought to a called session of General Conference in 2017 or 2018. We would leave it to the commission to think through whether to have two or three new bodies formed if division became a live option. If we wanted to be precise we would call this the General Commission on Separation option; but for mercy's sake let's call it simply the division option.

TRADITIONALIST   I like the notes of precision and realism here. I think we would have to see a bloodbath at the next General Conference for this to emerge.

EVANGELICAL   Here is a fourth option. The progressives win outright and manage to eliminate all the language in the current *Book of Discipline* that they dislike. I know that this is extremely unlikely given that progressives are much more likely to go for the third way option and either live with that for the foreseeable future or go back to work and finish their agenda. Let's call this the comprehensive progressive option.

TRADITIONALIST   Is there a fifth option?

EVANGELICAL   Yes. The fifth option is a variation on your deadlock option. After General Conference fails to make progress in any direction, individual congregations begin to pull out across the denomination. This would be a very messy business. Maybe they would simply go it alone; or maybe they would form a loose association or denomination (an option which could indeed happen, given our current regulations). I suspect that this could well be an option for some of the bigger mega-churches; and if it was exercised it could have very serious consequences for the finances of many of our Annual Conferences. So let's call this the withdrawal option.

TRADITIONALIST   Is there anything to add?

EVANGELICAL   At the risk of getting too complicated I can think of a variation of the third way option. In this instance, a set of amendments are introduced that would actually prepare for division down the road. One could imagine evangelicals and others taking the third option as a step in the right direction, but embracing it only because it would be the most likely way of securing a version of the division option. It would, of course, be a high-risk move to make. Moreover, it does not fit with the desire of most evangelicals to eschew dissimulation and deception. Those folk who love the intrigue and subplots of politics might well be ready to gamble on such a move.

TRADITIONALIST   Who knows what will happen up ahead, but overall I like the way you lay out the options.

EVANGELICAL   As my last option makes clear, what is really new in all this is the effort to move to a third option. I must confess that I did not see this coming. I certainly took note of the numbers when the resolution to agree to disagree failed at the last General Conference, but I did not anticipate a fresh formulation which really had serious content and that would so quickly be picked up in centrist and evangelical circles.

TRADITIONALIST   Frankly, I was in much the same boat on this one. Come to think of it, we should not be surprised. United

Methodists at heart are very good people. We do not like conflict and we hate division. Both of these virtues are burned into our souls. We have amazing resilience in getting along despite the fact that we have incredible diversity if you look at our church over the last hundred years or so. I love this about our people. Somehow we manage to get along and many of us sustain deep friendships across our divisions. We all know this goes back to John Wesley, of course, with his wonderful sermons on avoiding bigotry and embracing a catholic spirit. There are those who really see this as the virtue of virtues of our tradition. What makes United Methodism so wonderful is that we welcome everyone. When it comes to the current crisis you can see why this is the default position of so many across our church. We want to be friends of all and the enemy of none. Our calling card in the culture is that we see our differences as a virtue and not as a vice. Other great denominations have already ended up divided, but surely, it will be said, we are better than division. We can provide a genuinely new way of being church in a culture riddled with division, disharmony, and rancor. So you can understand the great appeal of a third way.

EVANGELICAL   I do indeed understand this and readily testify that the same blood beats in my own veins. We can add that at heart we do not like disruption. We are a people who work by incremental change rather than by radical reform. We have a whole raft of checks and balances that prevent any one group getting the upper hand, even though we know that up the line in the establishment committees and in institutions like the seminaries the progressive are exceptionally effective in pressing forward their agenda. One bishop described our publishing house as "progressive struggling to be fair." Most of us have all learnt to live with pressing on with our agendas but still refraining from crossing a line which acts as a curb on our more disruptive instincts. In a way we are all moderates at heart. We allow for revolution in extreme cases, but we are very reluctant revolutionaries. Even with all the barking, at the end of the day we would much prefer to wag our tails. We are afraid that folk who bark will bite us and we will do all in our power to keep things quiet and under rational control.

TRADITIONALIST   This is all very well and good until the tail starts wagging the dog!

EVANGELICAL   But everyone thinks it is somebody else's tail that is wagging the dog! In their more honest moments we all appear to think that we are losing and that the other side is winning. Maybe it is time to rework this metaphor and have the dog start barking for a change. My dogs do this when they sense there is danger at the door. Sometimes there really is danger at the door!

TRADITIONALIST   The danger at the moment is that folk will fail to see the problems inherent in the third way. I think both of us are pretty clear about this. It is time we set about sorting through why this is not the innocent option that its proponents think it is.

EVANGELICAL   So let's try and think this through. You promised earlier to tackle the issues.

Some Throat-Clearing

TRADITIONALIST   Getting clarity on what is before us is far from easy. This is generally the case with third ways that claim to take us above and beyond the extremes that folk in the third way invariably invoke. Let me immediately grant that I have no quarrel with the intentions of Reconciler and Pietist. I would gladly be first in line in lauding their gifts and graces. As we proceed, however, we need to bear in mind three considerations that can easily be forgotten or cleverly concealed. First, both of them are now revisionists when it comes to the canonical teaching of The United Methodist Church on sexuality and marriage. They are not neutral observers or impartial judges; they are partisans-in-the-making if not fully fledged partisans in the dispute about gay marriage and gay ordination. Second, what is essentially at stake is a local option, the position basically adopted by some other churches which have changed official moral teaching on gay marriage over recent years. So we have a track record elsewhere on how things play themselves out. The track record is that by degrees the progressive agenda becomes the official position. The challenge comes in sorting out what to do with the version of the local option specifically designed for United Methodism. Immediately we enter a grey area where confusion is likely to abound.

EVANGELICAL   And we know that having grey areas is a hallmark of the Hamiltonians in favor of the third way. If we stay at this level one group will managed to get its way for it is clear that not everybody thinks it good to treat the issues before us as grey.

The third way which is not a third way

TRADITIONALIST   Let's focus on the initial material content of the third way. Its proponents say that we should agree to disagree. At one level this is perfectly clear. Agreeing to disagree is a time-honored way of describing what we often do when we find ourselves at odds with others. It is a clear platitude of common sense. Yet it conceals as well as reveals. The real message this slogan sends is that our church is decidedly unclear in its stance on marriage and homosexual practice. It is as clear as anything can be that we cannot reach agreement on the substantial issues before us. So in the use of the very same set of words we have clarity and lack of clarity. Yet we are still not out of the woods. For consider what the third option actually means. It means that certain groups within the church are officially permitted to conduct same-sex marriages, for example. This means that same sex-marriages are entirely legitimate within the official teaching and practices of The United Methodist Church. So now we uncover the real truth of the matter: if we accept the third way it will have been officially decreed that same-sex marriage is entirely legitimate morally and theologically. So the third way can be read at one and the same time as agreeing to disagree on same sex marriages, being unclear on same-sex marriage and thus treating it as a grey area, and being patently clear that we legitimize same sex marriages.

EVANGELICAL   I suppose this is one reason why the third way is initially so attractive. You can read the same proposal and come away with whatever reading best fits your initial intuitions.

In reality folk with very different convictions can sign on because it is systematically ambiguous in its content. There is unseen equivocation. You can shift from seeing it as clear about agreeing to disagree, to thinking of it as upholding a grey area and thus unclear, and then find yourself landed with a full-scale legitimizing of same-sex marriage. No wonder it is so easy initially to get drawn into it as an irenic way forward only to find that the attraction is utterly superficial and hollow when you look more deeply.

TRADITIONALIST   Exactly. It is illuminating to go back at this point and look at the matter when it first came to the floor of General Conference at Atlanta in 1972. The Social Principles Study Committee brought forward a resolution that ran as follows. I brought a copy so you could see for yourself.

> *Human Sexuality.* - We recognize that sexuality is a good gift of God, and we believe persons may be fully human only when that gift is acknowledged and affirmed by themselves, the church, and society. We call persons to disciplines that lead to the fulfillment of themselves, others, and society in the stewardship of this gift. Medical, theological, and humanistic disciplines should combine in a determined effort to understand human sexuality more completely.

Although men and women are sexual beings whether or not they are married, sex between a man and woman is to be clearly affirmed only in the marriage bond. Sex may become exploitative within as well as outside marriage. We reject all sexual expressions which damage or destroy the humanity God has given us as birthright and we affirm only that sexual expression which enhances that same humanity in the midst of diverse opinion as to what constitutes that enhancement. Homosexuals no less than heterosexuals are persons of sacred worth, who need the ministry and guidance of the church in their struggles for human fulfillment, as well as the spiritual and emotional care of fellowship which enables reconciling relationships with God, with others, and with self. Further, we insist that all persons are entitled to have their human and civil rights ensured.

What is fascinating about this resolution is that it leaves open the option of affirming sexual relations in the non-heterosexual community so long as the sexual expression involved enhances our divinely given humanity. As to what that humanity involves then the best that can be offered is that there is diversity of opinion as to what constitutes the enhancement of humanity. Notice how the diversity angle was in play right from the start of the debate. Within certain vague boundaries you could read into it whatever you liked.

EVANGELICAL   It sounds as if sex is to be seen as a good indoor sport where anything goes so long as everyone involved gives consent and no one gets hurt.

TRADITIONALIST   Many delegates saw the latter part of the resolution as a reflection of the sexual revolution of the sixties and thus a serious departure from the teachings of the Christian tradition. They could see immediately that it really favored the progressive agenda as it was developing back then. One delegate, Thomas Reavley, then a Justice on the Supreme Court of Texas, was not very confident that anything presented would end the deadlock. Many others shared his pessimism. Yet the deadlock was broken when Don Hand, a young lawyer from Southwest Texas, who was attending his first General Conference, went to the microphone and proposed an amendment. In the end, the General Conference approved the substitution of a comma for the period at the very end and added the clause, "though we do not condone the practice of homosexuality and consider the practice incompatible with Christian teaching."

Many things stand out in this addition to the original resolution, but for my purposes what stands out is the clarity of the church's position. It is clear in what it has to say and it is clear on the status of what it says. It is clear on the content of its moral judgment; and it is clear on the official standing of its moral judgment. Delegates left the General Conference knowing where The United Methodist Church stood; so too did the press and outside observers; so did its advocates and opponents; so too did members and observers across the world. One District Superintendent told Don Hand immediately afterwards that his interventions had just saved twelve churches on his District from leaving United Methodism.

EVANGELICAL   Even back then the diversity card was being played as a way of avoiding the hard decisions that had to be made. Happily folk saw immediately what was at stake. It is much more difficult to see that with the current effort to make a virtue of diversity by those committed to the third way.

TRADITIONALIST   The core issue at the end of the day is very basic. Will The United Methodist Church stand by its long-standing vision of traditional marriage or will it canonically legitimize same-sex marriage? The third way clearly opts for the second alternative. Yet it seeks to conceal this decision by pretending to rise above the so-called extremes in the church. It does not offer a third way at all. It is progressive at its very core. This is not a middle position; it is a vote in favor of the progressive agenda.

EVANGELICAL   This is certainly helpful. It is tempting to leave this point in place and change the subject. However, I think a lot of folk are not at all sure why they should not in the end go with this subtle version of the progressive agenda. Many of them will not think for a moment that they are endorsing the gay agenda. They are just being fair and tolerant. Alternatively, they may think that there is something fishy but they do not know what. Given that their basic motto is safety first they bury their doubts and go with the promissory note that this option really is fair and tolerant.

TRADITIONALIST   I think 'devious' would be a better way to describe the agenda, even though I am not convinced that those behind it want to be devious. They may well be taken in by their own rhetoric at this point and simply fail to see what they are actually doing. Yet you are right to take the conversation a step further at this point and come clean on why I oppose the progressive agenda whatever form it may take in legislation. Will you permit me to be more direct?

EVANGELICAL   Of course.

Restating what is at Issue

TRADITIONALIST   The presenting issue is perfectly clear and we can put it directly to our own informed conscience. Each person must speak for themselves initially. We can pose the question initially as follows: Do I think that The United Methodist Church should approve of sodomy, same-sex marriage, and gay ordination? My answer to this question is no. If you ask me why, then, I would need to rehearse a complex network of arguments that are well known in the literature. I have nothing to add to that material; the evidence is essentially all in; and I am clear in my own mind on where I should stand as a Christian disciple and as a Christian theologian. The crucial consideration hinges on our Lord's teaching on marriage. I am trained in epistemology and could take you right now on a long detour to underwrite this deep conviction, but that would miss the essential point. I think that Jesus of Nazareth is the Son of God; He is Lord of my fragile and sinful life; not for a moment can I envisage any attempt on my part to correct or improve on his teaching. I could supplement this with a whole raft of additional considerations from divine revelation as enshrined in scripture and from other sources that would be important in a full-dress defense of my answer. However, in a way they are superfluous.

EVANGELICAL   I can see why you are zeroing in on our Lord's teaching on marriage. However, you are no doubt aware that even that is subject to all sorts of interpretation that would treat it as not ruling out same-gender marriages. The bottom line is that your opponents will claim that so long as Jesus does not explicitly say that same-gender marriage is wrong, they are in the clear as far as the teaching of Jesus is concerned.

TRADITIONALIST   I am indeed aware of this move. But notice a couple of things. First, this will also mean that other multiple-partner marriages will also be allowed on this reading. So it will not rule out polyandry, or even three persons of any gender getting married. We have no explicit prohibition of these on the part of Jesus. Second, the standard being assumed here is an ad hoc standard brought in to blunt the force of the teaching of our Lord. Think of all the sins that are not explicitly prohibited by Jesus. You can make your own list. Where does Jesus say explicitly that incest is wrong? Interestingly, this pseudo- standard was developed by some folk at the Reformation and it wreaked havoc in a host of moral lives. Richard Hooker is great on this issue. Finally, I never said that the wild human intellect in search of justification would not find a way around a plain reading of our Lord's teaching or anything else that does not fit with their moral stance. It is surely enough that this is an entirely responsible and viable reading of what he says. In the end each reader will have to face the music on this issue for themselves. I have had colleagues in my own annual conference who simply said Jesus got it wrong. At the very least, this is an honest response that avoids the fancy footwork one occasionally comes across.

EVANGELICAL   So I suppose the next question is this: Should The United Methodist Church provide explicit, official teaching that upholds the traditional vision of Christian marriage?

TRADITIONALIST   Exactly! And the answer is obvious: it should do so. After all, Jesus is Lord of his church. Any effort to depart from his teaching or to correct his teaching is simply out of the question. I hold that the teaching of Jesus is clear on this matter; so the official teaching of the church should be clear. We can add other considerations that would provide additional support for this contention. Whether we like it or not, this is the contested issue of our day, so it would show a lack of courage to duck it. Moreover, given that both members and outsiders think that this is a substantive rather than trivial moral question with serious ramifications for them in their lives and the societies they inhabit, they deserve a clear answer on where we stand officially. Furthermore, given that walking away from a clear answer would send a distinct signal that The United Methodist Church had changed its position and abandoned centuries of Christian wisdom, there really is little place for obfuscation and wiggle room in its public teaching. And of course, given the firm convictions you and I have arrived at, we all want to know where our church stands. I think she should uphold the position on marriage that has been in place since its beginning in its liturgies, its tacit teaching, and then in its formal decision at the General Conference in 1972.

EVANGELICAL   But the third way asserts that you can hold to your convictions with integrity and a good conscience? You can be a member of that part or unit of United Methodism that holds your views. This option would appear to give us all we want.

TRADITIONALIST   Exactly there is the sleight of hand and the opening that Reconciler and his associates seek sincerely to utilize to win over the middle. I am tempted to use the word 'exploit' but that would be neither fair nor felicitous. Put simply, it is exactly at this point that the lack of clarity becomes important to expose afresh. It starts out by affirming as the default position the standard vision of marriage. So it looks as if we are in good shape in terms of our official stance as a church. But then we immediately discover that the official position in terms of default teaching in not a clear answer; it is a qualified answer. This is exactly the point that the original move on agreeing to disagree made abundantly clear. Agreeing to disagree means that one is clear on that proposition, the proposition that we should agree to disagree. It hides the fact that one is insisting that the church in its official teaching is not clear, cannot be clear, and should not be clear on the proposition that sodomy, gay-marriage, and gay ordinations are morally unacceptable. It treats it as a contested grey area. But then when we look closer we discover that The United Methodist Church by allowing the opt-out for various units actually endorses same sex-marriage and all that that entails. As I noted earlier we move from apparent clarity that is in favor of traditional marriage, to lack of clarity in which it is treated as a grey area, and then finally we get the ultimate truth that The United Methodist Church legitimizes same-sex marriage. For me this is essentially the end of the story. This is where the spade is turned for the first and last time; it is where one must fish or cut bait; it is where I get off the train as a matter of theological and spiritual integrity.

EVANGELICAL   Can you state what is at issue more succinctly?

TRADITIONALIST   Yes. It is a ruinous mistake for any church to endorse directly or indirectly a vision of marriage that clearly contradicts that of our Lord and Savior Jesus Christ. To put the matter in terms of theological and moral conscience: I cannot and will not be part of a church that departs in this radical manner from the special revelation given to us in the Gospel. Others can and will differ from me on this; so be it. I am cannot and will not join them in an act of moral and theological heresy if not apostasy of this magnitude.

EVANGELICAL   The stakes are really high for you at this point.

A Historical Perspective

TRADITIONALIST   Indeed they are. Let me try a different way to state the gravity of what is at issue. Think of three really crucial periods in the history of the church. In the fourth century the church was on the brink of losing the theological content of the Gospel in the Arian controversy. At issue was a true account of the doctrine of God as developed in her teaching on the Trinity. At the Reformation, the church was in danger of losing the theological content of the Gospel in the controversy over justification by faith through grace. Happily this has now been virtually resolved as a result of intense ecumenical work. In the nineteenth century the church was in danger of losing divine revelation as the crucial ground of its moral and theological teaching. You tend to put it as a debate about the authority of scripture but the real debate was about the loss of divine revelation and its displacement by various wobbly accounts of reason and experience.

EVANGELICAL   We are really in deep agreement on this last point despite our different terms of reference.

TRADITIONALIST   Now here is the hard truth that must be faced. Today we face a similar crisis to the crises we faced in the fourth, the sixteenth, and the nineteenth centuries. This time the issue is both theological and moral. We are in the midst of a crisis where we are in danger of losing the treasures of our moral tradition enshrined in the church's wisdom about marriage. Equally,

115

we face the fatal danger of losing a critical element in the church's doctrine of creation. The crisis is a crisis of theological and moral nerve. Of course, I distinguish here between moral and theological only to be as clear as I can. They are in fact deeply connected but let that pass. The moral storm center is the church's vision of marriage; and the theological storm-center is the church's doctrine of creation and her doctrine of divine revelation. We have never faced anything like this before; the stakes are utterly analogous to what we faced in the fourth century, in the sixteenth century, and in the nineteenth century. This is not just one more bump in the road; it is a fork in the road.

EVANGELICAL   If I were to make this case then I would be accused of upping the ante in the debate so as to justify separation as a possible option. I would be accused of rationalization, of looking for justification for a position already arrived on other grounds.

TRADITIONALIST   Indeed you would, for the separation option causes folk to reach for anything that will keep it off the table. You will note that it is not an objection that can be lodged against me. As I reflect on what is happening with churches splitting left and right, I am convinced that we have to take the measure of this development much more seriously than we might at first allow. We need to face this head-on: what is at stake is heresy or apostasy.

EVANGELICAL   This is going to be a very hard sell given the current narratives running in our heads.

TRADITIONALIST   True indeed. The standard narrative is short and sweet. Mainline Christians in North America initially failed on slavery, failed on racism, failed on segregation, and failed on women's ordination. However, there was always a prophetic minority who saw the light and in time corrected the terrible mistakes we made. Now it is our turn to play our part in the great drama of history on the full inclusion of gays and their many associates. Even those on your side of the aisle find it hard not to take this story seriously. The story has another attractive feature: it fits the turn to moralism and sentimentality that are two of the favorite pastimes of Methodists. It can get the emotional and moral juices running at high speed in the way stories of conversion used to do during our times of revivalism. Or in the way the civil rights marches did in the nineteen sixties. I have seen grown men and women weep in full sight of God and everybody when the drama was tacitly invoked.

EVANGELICAL   I feel the force of this narrative myself. As do the vast majority of our leaders, not least our bishops.

TRADITIONALIST   You have to feel sorry for our bishops at times. Their default position is to avoid drama at all costs. The progressives have monopolized that end of our human sensibilities. The progressive bishops know exactly what buttons to push to get the drama up and running; they are fearless in public whatever their reservations may be in private; you have to admire them. So the rest of our leaders run to the middle as fast as possible. They have a salt lust for the middle even if they are progressive in their private judgments. They immediately think of safety first. Stick to the center. Keep the lights on. Watch your step. Keep an eye on the rear-view mirror. Never get off the beaten track. Be careful about what you say. Be moderate. Don't rock the boat. No thrills and spills here, please. Don't scare the horses. These are their mottos in a day of crisis such as we have never seen before. These are their blankets and insulators and insurance policies against reality. This is a religion of false comfort and ease in Zion. They think that all that is at stake is a bad case of a toothache rather than a slow but fatal disease. It is exactly this kind of default position which will ruin us in the end. It is the last thing we need given the challenge we face. The current crisis involves the kind of stark either/or that we have schooled ourselves to avoid. Believe me I understand this outlook. In sunny days when all is relatively bright and there is little prospect of a storm, something like it should be our default position. Now that the hurricane is upon us, it is disastrous.

EVANGELICAL   I can see how much getting the story right matters to you. To come back more strictly on topic, is there anything beyond these considerations of basic principle that carries the day for you?

A Raft of Subsidiary Considerations

TRADITIONALIST In terms of opening and shutting the case for myself, yes. But I am not prepared to leave it there. Then next question can be framed as follows. Would the decision to go with the third way alter irrevocably the essential character of United Methodism? I answer that it would. Here is my laundry list of reasons. First, it would turn us essentially towards a Congregational network of associations and congregations rather than a united connection standing together to evangelize the world and witness to the truth of the faith. Second, it would be a radical departure from our norms of doctrine. Third, it would undermine the place of General Conference as the final court in resolving issues of controversy for the General Conference would essentially have abdicated its responsibility and walked away from its constitutional mandate. Finally, it would also end any remaining place there would be informally for John Wesley being our father in God in the faith.

EVANGELICAL And?

TRADITIONALIST As a matter of practice it would show that the United Methodism Church is prepared to yield to a well-orchestrated campaign of bullying, intimidation, and agitation that has abandoned the place of reason and due process in its ethos and in its deliberative councils. Formally, we might repeat the shibboleths of our ethos and polity; by our actions we would have revealed that we have lost our nerve and have yielded to persistent, aggressive emotionalism and political theatre.

EVANGELICAL Aren't you ignoring the amount of ink spilled on attempting to persuade us that the progressive position is correct?

TRADITIONALIST Not at all. My point is that our progressives have only fitfully believed in following the evidence where it leads and in seeking to persuade the church by rational means. They have singularly failed to persuade the church where it really counts, that is, at General Conference. Hence the turn to use non-rational means to bring us to heel. While most folk reject self-immolation as an option, a tragedy that folk on all sides lament, the tactics become essentially political and ideological.

EVANGELICAL   Is there more to be said?

TRADITIONALIST   Indeed there is. There are excellent reasons why in time the church, ancient and modern, adopted ways of resolving controversial questions in the highest courts of the church. These questions require attentive investigation and well-crafted legislation. To shift these decisions down the line will create unnecessary havoc throughout the life of the church. There is no fool-proof solution to this problem, but wisdom has long declared that we put the whole church at risk by forfeiting the virtue of keeping this at the level of General Conference. If we go down the pathway of the third way we open the door to such havoc. Evangelicals should do everything in their power to avoid this development in Annual Conferences and local congregations in any solution they bring forward.

EVANGELICAL   This will not be easy because any plan of separation may well involve a similar risk. However, events have a way of getting folk to grow up and deal with them like adults. I suppose on your view if it came to separation and we had to have decisions down the line we would enter a world of appalling but maybe unavoidable tragedy.

TRADITIONALIST   You capture my mind precisely. In terms of content the third way proposals are at present radically incomplete. To date we have been given no detailed account of what will be in place for those who reject the proposed norms of homosexual unions. Given the obvious diversity in sexual orientation and given the more recent arguments that reject heterosexual monogamy as the norm for marriage, this is a serious piece of unfinished business for all on the progressive side. I am sure folk are working on this problem but for now there is a massive lacuna here that I am not sure Reconciler has recognized much less addressed it. It will not do, for example, to go back to 1972 and reintroduce the vague generalities about not damaging but enhancing the humanity given to us by God in creation. It would be a hallmark of bad and ill-formed canon law that these detailed questions are not addressed. There should be no small print lurking anywhere in any document; the proposals need to be transparent and open.

EVANGELICAL   What about the reception of the local option?

TRADITIONALIST   First, this proposal will not bring an end to our battles. As many have noted, it will mean serious conflict for thousands of congregations. Second, this is a short-term solution that will not survive for long. For a time there might be a truce; but only for a time. What is now a permitted option will in time become the default position that allows minority dissent; then it will become a moral imperative. Third, if we were ever to get clear legislation that would seek to keep the peace between the various units, we would need an army of enforcers to keep the progressives from pressing on to final victory. No such enforcers exist. Fourth, the public reading and perception of this way forward would be trumpeted as a victory for the progressive wing of the church. You can just see the headlines on the evening news and national newspapers. They would in fact be telling the truth. Fifth, it would create enormous difficulties for the witness of conservative United Methodists inside and outside the United States. 'Enormous' is much too weak a term; 'devastating' would be more accurate. Sixth, it would mean that those who read the situation akin to what I have outlined would have to grin and bear it, leave, or find a way to found a new denomination that in all likelihood would be small and wounded from the outset.

EVANGELICAL   What would it mean for you personally?

TRADITIONALIST   Frankly for me, and for a lot of people I know, everything is at stake.

Dialogue VIII

Focusing on the Future

PIETIST   I am so pleased that you all agreed to come back together again. I was beginning to fear that our use of my round table was beginning to falter.

TRADITIONALIST   I am not sure much can be accomplished but I am all for getting as much clarity as possible so that we know where we stand, at least in public.

RECONCILER   I am in much the same situation, although, to be frank, I am more interested in getting a consensus out of the next General Conference on our third way. We can then go home to our conferences, enact our own convictions, and get on with our own ministries.

TRADITIONALIST   Speaking of consensus, I hope we can pass a resolution that sets a moratorium on all debate about sexuality for the next twenty years. We have had forty years of discussion with a clear outcome and it is time to get a rest from the shenanigans that we have had to endure.

PROGRESSIVE   You can be assured that such a resolution will be opposed root and branch by our side. We shall not give up until we have full inclusion for all our gay brothers and sisters. That will also mean we will be lobbying for gays to be appointed to the big churches, to be selected as district superintendents, and to be elected as bishops. I can also envisage days set apart for public apologies for the harm done to our gay communities. So any advances at the next General Conference are essentially steps in a wider campaign that will end discrimination.

EVANGELICAL   I fully understand why you find yourself adopting such a course of action. You understandably want to follow your convictions wherever they lead. I am in the same boat. You surely understand that we would have to oppose your agenda every step of the way. So you can surely also understand why a clean division with an equitable sharing of the assets is one way forward if not the best way forward. We are tired fighting an interminable war. We are not interested in debating sexual morality and related issues for another forty years. It is time to find a way forward where there are no winners and losers.

RECONCILER   It is our third way that will give us that outcome. Your plan means the end of The United Methodist Church and the creation of two or three new churches. If that is not a loss then I do not know what a loss is.

TRADITIONALIST   We are really beginning to stake out how we see our potential futures. Perhaps we should move to this and see where we are.

PROGRESSIVE   I am happy to begin. Of course, there are other issues we could discuss. I would love to know what Evangelical will do with all the LGBTQUIA folk who are already in his churches.

EVANGELICAL   They are already welcomed and received in the way that Christ has welcomed us. We have worked on these issues for years, but I doubt if you would be interested. We are not the mean nasty Christians that you think we are; we have our own principled way of tackling the pastoral and moral issues at stake. For my part, I would love to know if Progressive plans to send advocates and agitators into our churches in order to disrupt our work.

PROGRESSIVE   That is not something we can control. People are people and they will do whatever they think is best. We have no official stance on such action one way or another. However, I can readily imagine some of our people being committed to a form of evangelism where the victims of homophobia deliberately visit your churches in order to put a name and a face to the people you are abusing and thus begin the process of transformation. The church really needs to be told the truth and called to repentance.

RECONCILER   I would love to know how Traditionalist would tackle the demands of education, given his obsession with past tradition. As you know I greatly value the training I got from a network of older liberal scholars who really were honest about the relevant evidence and gave us room to think for ourselves.

TRADITIONALIST   I think you and I would be closer on this than you think. I assume that you are profoundly unhappy with the progressive effort to blackball those in the academy who disagree with them when it comes to appointments and tenure. We need top-rank, genuine educational institutions that pursue truth and knowledge rather than operate as devious schools of indoctrination. Good education takes tradition radically seriously, but this would require a treatise in philosophy of education to elaborate. I am not sure you really want this here.

EVANGELICAL   I am with traditionalist in the need for top-notch university schools of theology but I think we also need good conservative confessional schools which have their own part to play in the ecology of education. Actually, I would love to know how we plan to relate to the wider culture in the West. We seem to have two options when it comes to the new forms of civil rights that are being invented: be marginalized and criminalized as bigots or coopted as advocates for radical reform.

PIETIST   As for me, I would like to have each of us spell out our moral and theological vision of sexual morality given the new situation in which we find ourselves. We really have not given serious attention to the deeper issues involved. We seem to prefer shouting at each other across the ramparts and then adopting the first account that fits with our political agenda.

TRADITIONALIST   If we keep this up we will never finish. We all know that there is more at stake than the presenting issue that gets all the attention and that the media are all too keen to highlight. So I wonder if we could not go back to Progressive who agreed to lead off in saying what we can about the future we would like for our church. As we proceed we can ask questions of each other and see if that helps to get clarity.

A Fully Inclusive Church

PROGRESSIVE   Our goal is simple. On one hand, we want an end to the harmful language and discrimination; on the other, we want the full inclusion of gays in every level of the church's life. This fits with our vision of United Methodism as a mainline Protestant denomination that is open to necessary change and bold enough to step up and make necessary changes.

TRADITIONALIST   Is that all there is?

PROGRESSIVE   For the moment, yes. Sufficient unto the day are the troubles thereof. Of course, this is one element in a wider vision that sees United Methodism as progressive in other areas as well. So we are committed to social action, especially for the poor and marginalized. We reject fundamentalism and believe in critical investigation of scripture. We are open to well-considered changes in worship, polity, church administration, and pretty much everything across the board in the life and work of the church. We are committed to science and the life of reason. Indeed we see our church as a haven for folk who have abandoned Christianity because it is so narrow and judgmental. We think that our church has great days ahead of us as we join with the mainstream of North American church life and offer a place to be loved. We also want a place where you can think for yourself and be supported in your unique intellectual and spiritual development.

EVANGELICAL   You are aware that this is a recipe for decline, as all the evidence shows.

PROGRESSIVE   Things may look bad at the moment but we are addressing real needs and developments in our culture. There are lots of individual progressive churches that thriving. These can act as models for us. Once we win the war within United Methodism then we can devote attention to getting our message out and drawing in a whole new generation who want spirituality but are dead-set against organized religion. We will be able to persuade them that organized religion is not as bad as they think it is. In any case we are not sold on success as a criterion of success. We are perfectly happy to be a prophetic minority. The best scholarship is on our side and most of our seminaries are on board with our agenda. Of course, they cannot say so officially, but that is fine. Everybody knows where they stand and that is what matters.

PIETIST   Do you think that you could incorporate more of John and Charles Wesley into the agenda?

PROGRESSIVE   This is not a problem, provided you place the Wesley brothers in their context first. You cannot microwave their beliefs and practices. We live in the twenty-first century and not in the eighteenth century. In his day the big challenge was guilt. Folk were overburdened with a sense of guilt which was aptly met by the message of early Methodism. Today folk are more likely to be overwhelmed by loss of meaning at the top end of society and by grinding poverty at the lower levels. We have to rethink the message in order to meet them where they are. We need to tackle the structural problems that are central to people's lives, like, poverty, racism, oppression, discrimination, education, and the like. We love the way we have figured out to do mission trips inside and outside the United States. John Wesley is a wonderful inspiration in all of this. He was really into experience and transformation.

TRADITIONALIST   Do you have a doctrine of the church that fits your vision of Methodism?

PROGRESSIVE   I have not given much thought to this, but I suppose we do. We certainly know what we are against. We are not a confessional church that puts much store by correct doctrine, least of all, ancient doctrine. Our teaching is driven by experience and by action. The intellectual content changes with changing intellectual and cultural changes. The same goes for liturgy, sacraments, and church order, even though we have folk who are as keen to be bishop as is the case in other sections of United Methodism. One observer has suggested that at heart we are committed to a church of true believers, given our passion for social justice and inclusion. But we see true believers as believers in action. It would probably be more apt to see us as a movement

125

that seeks to remake the church from below. That gives us a real kinship with early Methodism. Moreover, we think that God is present everywhere so that everyone has to find their own path to salvation. For us this means we meet God through Christ, but other ways work effectively for other people. I suppose church is where people have discerned God's action in their personal lives but most of all in history and have joined in that action of liberation and justice. That church is pretty much without borders and known only to God.

EVANGELICAL   And where does the Bible fit into all this?

PROGRESSIVE   Everywhere. We follow the lectionary for the most part. Most of our preachers use it but not slavishly. Of course, we read it as an ancient text that has to be interpreted for today. Our focus is on its liberating power rather than see it as a book of doctrines and propositions.

A Centrist Church

RECONCILER   There is much in all of this that I can affirm. What I really want is a church where we learn to agree to disagree. This means working out a version of the local option that will be officially adopted and not imposed by any group, including the group I lead and represent. This will allow everyone to follow their conscience, including allowing me to enact my own agreement with the progressive agenda on gay marriage. Whether my own local church or Annual Conference will go along with me is an open question. I can and live with their decisions. My first concern is for the church as a whole rather than for my own personal views on gay marriage. I want to see United Methodism offer a unique vision of the Christian faith that transcends the current battles waged by extremists who ignore the vast number of people in the middle. We can be a model to other churches and to the world in dealing with contentious issues that constantly tear us apart. Some have called this the extreme center. However, I prefer to drop any language that can be associated with extremism. It is exactly the actions of extremists that have to be overcome by reaching for a position that goes beyond their ideological agendas. What is really at issue is getting it right officially on the delicate balance between unity and diversity. It is the diversity end of the dialectic that needs attention right now.

PROGRESSIVE   What about other elements in the progressive agenda?

RECONCILER   There will a yes or no depending on what is on offer. I say no to change in our orthodox doctrines. I say no to any vision that would inhibit our evangelistic work in reaching out and saving souls. I generally eschew the language of saving souls but I want to be clear that I stand on the need for genuine conversion. I am all in favor of retrieving the language of revival so long as we update it to fit our current situation. I suppose I come closest to you in reworking my earlier views on scripture. With you I much prefer to speak of the transforming power of scripture, although we may disagree on what exactly is transformative and what is not transformative. I could go on cataloguing what is at stake between us, but the main point really takes care of it. We hammer out together a way to live with our differences within a broad vision of what constitutes our unity.

PIETIST   This really fits with a vision of United Methodism that is thoroughly Wesleyan.

RECONCILER   Yes indeed. As Albert Outler taught us so brilliantly we are the church that works with a both/and rather than a stark either/or. So we are in favor of both evangelism and social action, of both scripture and tradition, of both reason and experience, of both formal and informal liturgies, of both faith and works, of both denominational loyalty and ecumenical allegiance, of both divine grace and genuine human agency, of both sacramental practice and private devotion, and of both intellectual innovation and apt conservation. We are a bridge church that holds the center between Catholic and Protestant, between Evangelical and Liberal, between Holiness and Pentecostal, between Orthodoxy and Revision, and hopefully between traditional marriage and gay marriage. It is absolutely crucial that this kind of irenic witness be kept alive for the future.

EVANGELICAL   And you really think that this is biblical?

127

RECONCILER   Yes indeed. Think of Acts 15 and look at how the church opened its doors to the Gentile converts who were not circumcised. She got beyond the extremes of hardline Jewish forms of Christianity and licentious forms of Gentile Christianity as we detect in Corinth. Paul fits our agenda perfectly once you exclude the material where he got it wrong on the will of God. He got it wrong on women and he got it wrong on homosexuality. Or to put it more carefully, he may have gotten these issues right in his context but we live in a radically different context and need to update our reading of his letters.

EVANGELICAL   So you are effectively a supersessionist when it comes to the relation between Israel and the church?

RECONCILER   If by that you mean that I think that Paul was right to break the boundaries of Judaism and that the New Testament church effectively becomes the New Israel that replaces the old, law-driven Israel, then I would agree. In the same way today we need to open up and expand the boundaries to those who in earlier generations were excluded and vehemently rejected. Another way to make the point is in terms of the Reformation. The church is always in the business of improvement and of updating its ancient heritage. We are *ecclesia semper reformanda,* as the Latin slogan puts it. Our Reformed cousins tend to be better at working things out intellectually but they tend to be brutal in imposing the new agenda on everybody. Given our heritage of revival and transformation we actually tend to be less brutal with one another despite the actions of our extremists. The Methodist way is to work things out together, to live and let live as long as possible and on as many issues as possible. I can even heartily sign on to that vision of the church that sees it as identified as those congregations where the pure Word of God is preached and the sacraments properly administered. The rub comes in sorting out what exactly is meant by the pure Word of God. Our challenge at the moment is to accept that we do not agree on the content of the pure Word of God. We must learn to take the challenge of purity as a challenge to live together with our disagreements rather than despite our disagreements. You can put this grandly by speaking of appropriate diversity but we all know what is at stake. There needs to be a proper balance between unity and diversity.

PIETIST   I can come in here in the middle and simply record that for the most part I am in agreement with Reconciler. My agenda is to operate as a sweet-smelling incense that holds up the crucial place of prayer and of holy conferencing around my round table.

TRADITIONALIST   I suppose it is now my turn.

PIETIST   The table is all yours, my friend.

The Church as the Church of the Holy Spirit

TRADITIONALIST   The easiest way to think of my vision of the future is to think of it as a strictly short-term vision. In fact I am skeptical of grand visions and ecclesiastical utopias. But I suspect I will not be able to keep the bigger picture at bay. I want to go back before the creation of The United Methodist Church into both the tradition of The Methodist Episcopal Church and The Evangelical United Brethren. I know that constitutionally this is exactly where our church stands but we took a wrong turn in the late sixties and early seventies when we bought Albert Outler's vision of United Methodism. He came within an ace of upending our constitution when he introduced all that material about the quadrilateral and pluralism. The damage is limited because all he got was a legislative amendment rather than the constitutional change he really wanted. We now know he reneged on this and accepted late in life that the only opponent he really respected, Robert Cushman of Duke, was right in opposing him. Cushman insisted that we should leave our doctrinal commitments as they were rather than add a statement which effectively made them into historical relics and landmarks.

RECONCILER   I would be interested in seeing the evidence for this change of heart and mind.

TRADITIONALIST   I can assure you that it is all there in his later papers at Perkins School of Theology, Southern Methodist University. The real problem, to be more precise, is that we tried an experiment in theological pluralism that was doomed from the outset. It was incoherent because pluralism cannot accommodate those who reject pluralism as a proposal about the nature of the church. This, of course, is so esoteric a point that it registers with very few observers. The more salient point is that pluralism is inescapably unstable. It only lasts so long as there are enough liberals who can hold things together above the competing voices that want to take over the table. In a way, the founding Father of United Methodism was Albert Outler just as John Wesley was the founding Father of early Methodism. Once he and his disciples disappear then the chaos below the surface gets exposed. Outler tended to see the church as a wonderful academic seminar where he sat at the top of the table, set the reading list, and had the first and last word. Pluralism goes with that intellectualist vision of the church. It now gets reworked in terms of holding various interests in balance or in terms of our being a society of friends. I see us as a real church complete with scriptures, doctrinal commitments, bishops, canon law, sacraments, and all the other elements that distinguish a church from a renewal movement or a fellowship group. This is what makes me a traditionalist. I think the church is constituted by a raft of materials, practices, and persons which are to be received as precious gifts of the Holy Spirit on the road to holiness. United Methodism and its originating bodies had its own unique way of articulating what this involved. It is one task of its contemporary theologians to spell all this out in a fresh way.

PIETIST   I really like your emphasis on the work of the Holy Spirit.

TRADITIONALIST   You tempt me to offer a quotation from Irenaeus. "Where the church is there is the Holy Spirit; and where the Holy Spirit is there is the church and fullness of grace and truth." I quote from memory, so I may be improving on excellence. It is the latter half of that quotation that is so important for us as United Methodists.

RECONCILER   So how do you read Acts 15?

TRADITIONALIST   I reject the idea that the church replaces

130

Israel. Paul was not a supersessionist who replaces Israel with the church as the New Israel. Paul was a Torah-observant Jew. He made room for Gentile converts not by rejecting a Messianic version of Judaism represented by Jewish converts but by allowing genuine diversity within the one body so that one could be fully Jewish and fully Gentile. If you were a Jew, you were obliged to stay a Jew, and if a Gentile a Gentile. We face the same challenge in reverse today with the fresh arrival of Messianic Judaism. They want us to give them space to be Jewish just as they gave us space to be Gentile.

RECONCILER   And just as I want us to provide space for those excluded today.

TRADITIONALIST   You generalize much too quickly. Paul won the day by showing that in creating space for Gentiles he was in line with the original covenant with Abraham. You cannot offer the same defense for your innovation. Your position involves a radical departure from the moral content of that covenant as developed in scripture and the life of the church. In fact, if you check the text of Acts 15 you specifically reject the conditions for unity insisted on by the Jerusalem Council. They are quite explicit about requiring the rejection of sexual immorality.

PIETIST   Can you come back to this claim that where the Holy Spirit is there is the church. This really warms my heart in ways that take me by surprise given our earlier disagreements. Can you say more?

TRADITIONALIST   Let me try a very quick taxonomy and then allow Evangelical to have his say. I see our bigger divisions within Christianity in a way that may indeed surprise you. There is the big 'C' Catholic and Orthodox option. Here they bet the store on the historical episcopate, on baptismal regeneration, on an exclusionary account of the Eucharist, and on a clerical hierarchy with or without Rome. I honestly think that Wesley began life with an Anglican version of this option and it failed him. The second option is Magisterial Protestantism. Here the gamut runs from Lutheran through Reformed through the many versions of the Baptist tradition. The core this time is to learn the original

131

languages and finally figure out what to believe and do, not least what to do by way of church ministry and polity. Methodism does not really fit here either for we do not believe that there is a normative church polity in scripture. We begin with the work of the Holy Spirit and effectively buy the slogan that where the Spirit is there is the church and the fullness of grace. This is why Acts 15 is indeed so important. It is the Spirit that creates and sustains the church; and it is the Spirit that equips the church with all the instruments of ministry and unity without which it simply descends into sectarian division and chaos. We were born in awakening, revival, and renewal. What Wesley did was reposition us as a third option where he understood Methodism as a fresh expression of Primitive Christianity that stretched beyond the New Testament era into the first centuries of the church's life.

EVANGELICAL   We have tended to treat Methodism as a variation on the Magisterial Protestant option. We are a church of the Word and not just a church of the Spirit.

TRADITIONALIST   We may not be far apart here but much hinges on the first step we take. It is not a matter of either/or in this instance; it is a matter of where we begin. The great creeds of the church name the work of the Spirit just before it speaks of the church; this is where I also begin. Note that I do not limit the work of the Spirit to the work of conversion and sanctification but carry that work over into the inspiration of scripture, the provision of order, the life of the sacraments, the offices and work of episcopacy, and the whole institutional life of the church. Will y'all permit one final footnote for my time is up?

PIETIST   Of course!

TRADITIONALIST   If you run this vision of the church forward from Wesley and not just run it back through the Reformation to the patristic period and to the early church, look at what emerges. Run it forward through revivals, the Holiness Movement, Pentecostalism, and on into the non-western world and you find the most vibrant form of Christianity in the contemporary world. In the short term we need to survive the efforts to make one final turn into mainline progressive Protestantism. We need to keep our nerve and look to see our treasures retrieved and upgraded by the genuinely fresh winds of the Spirit blowing across the world.

A New Global Wesleyan and Methodist Church

EVANGELICAL   The more you talk the more I find myself occupying similar if not identical terrain! In the short term I think it is time we really made plans to divide and abandon the false pluralism that has caused such havoc. Even if such a plan is rejected it can still be available for future generations to deploy. What is crucial is that we do not be taken for one more ride down a primrose path of empty platitudes about peace and reconciliation. We need a fresh articulation of who we are that is really owned by our people and that stops us going round and round in circles just to keep our vision afloat. In the short-term it will be rough; but once folk get over the initial shock and pain, they would be excited at what they would see. We need a real vision of hope that would put fire in their belly. In fact, the more I begin to think of a future that is really true to our deepest identity, the more excited I get by the moment! It would be a roller-coaster future, but at least it would be a future. It might even be that the withdrawal option would work if we are forced into it and if we give it serious attention. Clearly we are facing a whole new realignment within the contemporary Christian world. A good friend of mine pointed out some years ago that what we have been facing in the church is a third schism. The first schism was between East and West; the second was the schism in the West between Roman Catholic and Protestant. The third schism cuts across all the churches in the West, including the Roman Catholic Church. The core of the division is between those who want to hold to the classical faith of the church and those who no longer think it is credible. The latter want to revise the faith to fit with the changing trends of modern and postmodern culture. The modern move was to ditch the great doctrines of the faith, like, Trinity and Incarnation. The postmodern move is to ditch critical moral elements in the faith of the church. Progressive evangelicals think they can do this and still hold on to the great faith of the church.

PIETIST   I think you are wandering off topic.

EVANGELICAL   Take a step back in time with me for a moment. The revisionist liberals of the nineteenth century ditched the classical theological teaching of the church but kept the moral core. They would have blushed to hear what is now being proposed; they would have dismissed the current proposals on sex as an exercise in fornication. Some contemporary revisionists have already ditched the classical faith of the church and now want to ditch the moral faith of the church. Other contemporary revisionists want to hold on to the classical theological teaching of the church but ditch the classical moral teaching. As my mother would have said, at the end of the day they are all the one sow's pigs. Here is the payoff from this observation. Any new version of Methodism worth its salt should be thinking of where it will be fifty years from now. I can even see an exciting refurbished ecumenical engagement where we bring our own gifts and graces to the table and ditch that part of the tradition that has opted for the third schism in the church.

PIETIST   Can you stick to the agenda without rehearsing again your objections to the other alternatives?

EVANGELICAL   My apologies. It is hard to do this when you believe that your first obligation is to call the fire brigade and salvage what you can before the whole house goes up in fire. At the end of the day what I want is a new Global Methodist Church, the GMC. Our version of Methodism would start with what we currently have in terms of doctrine, polity, and discipline. We can even live with our mission statement of making disciples for the transformation of the world. We take the portion of the relevant assets that really fit this agenda and let the rest go. At the outset we would be global in nature, a matter of vital importance given the fires of the Holy Spirit at work outside the USA. To upgrade a saying of Wesley, "We need their heat and we all need light." So we can naturally own our heritage from the ancient church that Thomas Oden has brought to our attention (and given us the texts we need). We can also preserve the best in our Reformation heritage with its Wesleyan update. Equally, we can be fully open to the current amazing stirrings of the Holy Spirit sweeping across the growing churches of the global church. I like the move to express all this in terms of being open to all the gifts that the Holy Spirit wants to give to the Bride of Christ, but I want to make sure our thinking in this arena is normed by the revelation given in scripture.

TRADITIONALIST   I am with you in the way you capture how we should think of our norms. The EUB Confession of faith can help us here.

EVANGELICAL   There are other ways the EUB heritage can help us. It can help us to be less uptight about infant baptism. Their sense of flexibility would also allow us to think creatively of making much greater use of the sacrament of the Lord's Supper in homes and small groups. That heritage can encourage us to be far more proactive in improving our official doctrinal commitments and in really teaching this material with flair in our churches. Many of their bishops were in fact splendid teachers of the classical faith of the church. We would have, of course, also a publishing house that would really take up the challenge of doing the same rather than operating as progressive struggling to be fair. Of course, we will also need a really first rate GMC magazine available both in print and online.

TRADITIONALIST   I would like to add a footnote here. You begin with our own distinctive heritage, of course, but if you want to be global, why not open up to all the other Methodist bodies scattered through space and time. On the one hand, let's open our doors to those little churches like in Cuba and Ireland who would add their flavor to the mix as well as feel the strength that comes from being part of something much bigger. We could also begin conversations with those thriving units of Methodism in Latin America and Asia. On the other hand, we could look over the fence to our cousins among the Wesleyans, the Free Methodists, the Church of the Nazarene, the Salvation Army, and so on. We could begin with various orders of membership and see where the Holy Spirit might lead us over the next century.

EVANGELICAL   I would be all-in on this project but realistic about making progress. We have treated many of these churches with disdain and arrogance across the years so they will naturally and rightly be nervous. Some will have other agendas. We can be sure they will be worried about new forms of triumphalism operating despite the best intentions expressed. The initial effort would involve beginning with what we would already have in hand and going from there. Of course, I am assuming all through this that we will want to work in closest possible cooperation with other Christian churches that broadly share the great faith of the church and many of whom have been forced out by the coalition of radical and moderate progressives. We already have the networks in place to take up this kind of project.

PROGRESSIVE   I can see lots of diversity in your new Global Methodist Church but you really would kill pluralism once and for all.

EVANGELICAL   I suppose you are right about this. I am tempted to suggest that you really are doing the same, but let me avoid the temptation. We tried playing the pluralist cards back in the seventies and eighties but it was clear that pluralism did not really have room for our agenda. It was clear that the pluralism in play was a very restricted pluralism! We discovered that once you make orthodoxy one option in a cafeteria of options, it soon gets taken off the menu. Orthodoxy is not just one more option among others; we really think it is essential to the unity of the church. However, in a new church settling into some kind of refurbished orthodoxy will not be the top priority. Our top priority will be preaching the Gospel, saving souls, building up old and new converts, taking the faith into our communities in love and grace, planting new churches in places which have never heard the Gospel, and the like. This does not exclude other desirable goals like building hospitals and colleges and all the other kind of work that has been in Methodism from the beginning. However, we have never wavered from the first priority of seeing people come to the Savior and Lord of the church and the universe. We stand by Wesley's rule: You have nothing to do but to save souls and go not to those who need you but to those who need you most.

TRADITIONALIST   I like both the focus and the aggressively activist agenda you propose here.

EVANGELICAL   That agenda will also include a significant effort to take care of those many local congregations that are currently on life support. Maybe we need a whole new generation of itinerating evangelists and revivalists to bring new life to many of our rural churches which have been left to die on the vine. We need flexible experiments to see what might be done. Let's get some top notch preachers, a network of Mariachi bands, hire some buses, and get on the road again.

TRADITIONALIST   With you I really do think that if we weather the current storms we have a genuinely great future ahead of us.

PROGRESSIVE AND RECONCILER   We think that our visions for the future are even more attractive and exciting.

PIETIST   I suppose we have no other choice than to leave each other in the hands of the living God and let the future itself decide!

TRADITIONALIST   I do not share your pessimism at this point. This long and difficult dialogue has led me to see the crisis we face is an absolute Godsend. It has awakened us from our ecclesial smugness, our dogmatic slumbers, and our misplaced amiability. It has undone any persistent anxiety I may have had about the future. Even if I end up as a minority within a minority, I am convinced that the best days for our Methodist and Wesleyan heritage may well be ahead of us. We may have to slim down before we can grow again. We may be one of the least of the tribes of Israel, but we are still a tribe of a noble and wonderful household that will outlast the current trends and fashions.

Recently published by **Highland Loch Press:**

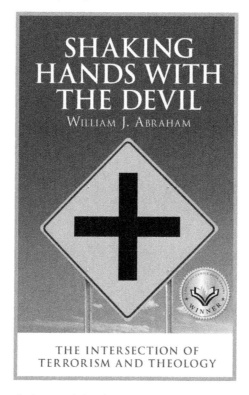

SHAKING
HANDS WITH
THE DEVIL
WILLIAM J. ABRAHAM

THE INTERSECTION OF
TERRORISM AND THEOLOGY

In the wake of 9/11 much has been written on terrorism. Some have examined the potential relation between religion and terrorism, few, if any, have studied the relation between theology and terrorism. In the latter case, the crucial issue is whether theology provides indirect or direct motivation and justification for terrorist acts. Drawing on his childhood and youth in Northern Ireland, William J. Abraham tackles the latter question head on. He argues that religious themes and practices play a pivotal indirect role in terrorism in Ireland and shows that theology plays a pivotal direct role in forms of Islamist terrorism. Hence current forms of terrorism cannot be fully understood without coming to terms with the crucial place of religion and theology in their origins and persistent existence.

This book is an eye-opener on terrorism and a rigorous theological response to the moral and spiritual challenges posed by one of the great evils of our times.

CPSIA information can be obtained at www.ICGtesting.com
Printed in the USA
LVOW04s1813111114

413107LV00003B/609/P